SPECTRUM

Math

Grade 4

School Specialty.
Publishing

Columbus, Ohio

Send all inquiries to:
School Specialty Publishing
8720 Orion Place
Columbus, OH 43240-2111

ISBN 0-7696-3704-3

4 5 6 7 8 9 10 POH 11 10 09 08

Table of Contents Grade 4

Table of Contents, continued

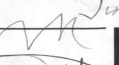

NAME _____

Check What You Know

Adding and Subtracting 1 and 2 Digits

Add or subtract.

	a	b	c	d	e	f
1.	35 + 3 38	25 +13 38	75 +24 99	13 +12 25	42 + 7 49	54 +33 87
2.	43 +24 67	54 + 5 59	63 +31 94	82 +16 98	32 +23 55	74 +15 89
3.	50 +33 83	95 + 2 97	32 +25 57	73 +25 98	56 +13 59	47 +32 79
4.	12 + 7 19	36 +12 48	55 +23 78	70 +19 89	92 + 4 96	54 +23 77
5.	45 – 04 41	75 –23 52	66 –14 52	95 –31 64	84 –22 62	25 –12 13
6.	49 –27 22	57 –46 11	39 –18 21	79 –27 52	27 – 6 21	88 –56 32
7.	65 –55 10	78 –33 45	54 –42 12	97 –26 71	29 –15 14	59 –48 11
8.	54 –23 31	29 –18 11	47 –37 10	99 –66 33	89 –27 62	36 –15 21

Check What You Know

SHOW YOUR WORK

Adding and Subtracting 1 and 2 Digits

Solve each problem.

9. Kai has 10 postcards from her cousin Alicia. She put them into her collection box with her other 46 postcards. How many postcards does Kai have in her box?

There are ___56___ postcards in her box.

9.
$$10$$
$$+46$$

10. Mr. Dimas has 15 new students in his fourth-grade class. He already has 21 students in the class. How many students are in Mr. Dimas's class?

There are ___36___ students in his class.

10.
$$15 \text{ new}$$
$$+21$$
$$36$$

11. There are 35 pages in Kendrick's science book. Last night, Kendrick read 14 pages. How many more pages does Kendrick have left to read?

There are ___21___ pages left to read.

11.
$$35$$
$$-14$$
$$21$$

12. Kono's father gave him 75 apples so he could pass them out to his friends. If Kono gave 43 away, how many apples does he have left?

There are ___32___ apples left.

12.
$$75 \text{ amps}$$
$$43$$
$$-32$$

13. Monica and Tania want to throw a surprise party for Rosa. They plan to send out 45 invitations. If Tania writes 24, how many invitations does Monica need to write?

Monica needs to write ___21___ invitations.

13.
$$45$$
$$24$$
$$21$$

14. Seki's soccer team is in the State Cup Tournament. There were 23 goals made in the entire tournament. Seki's team made 12 of them. How many goals were made by the other teams?

The other teams scored ___11___ goals.

14. $23-12=11$

999 999 **NAME** John 6/17/17

	Add the ones.	Add the tens.

```
addend  →    6      60        23       23        23
addend  →   +3     +30       +16      +16       +16
sum     →    9      90                  9        39
```

If 6 + 3 = 9, then 60 + 30 = 90.

Add.

	a	b	c	d	e	f
1.	11 + 8 **19**	10 +30 **40**	25 +14 **39**	81 +18 **99**	52 +17 **69**	74 +23 **97**
2.	10 +80 **90**	7 +2 **9**	15 + 4 **19**	7 +92 **99**	71 + 6 **77**	70 +10 **80**
3.	7 +22 **29**	20 +30 **50**	92 + 7 **99**	83 +16 **99**	46 +23 **69**	70 +20 **90**
4.	2 +41 **43**	30 +30 **60**	51 +48 **99**	34 +24 **58**	7 +22 **29**	20 +50 **70**
5.	30 +15 **45**	21 +21 **42**	7 +42 **49**	40 +40 **80**	56 +41 **97**	62 +17 **79**
6.	34 +34 **68**	60 +13 **73**	9 +30 **39**	4 +3 **7**	13 + 6 **19**	44 +33 **77**
7.	3 +32 **35**	5 +10 **15**	63 +24 **87**	71 +20 **91**	41 + 8 **49**	32 +30 **62**

Lesson 1.2 Subtracting 1- and 2-Digit Numbers

minuend ⟶ 9   90
subtrahend ⟶ −3   −30
difference ⟶ 6   60

If 9 − 3 = 6, then 90 − 30 = 60.

	Subtract the ones.	Subtract the tens.
53 −21	53 −21 2	53 −21 32

Subtract.

	a	b	c	d	e	f
1.	33 −12	43 −20	91 −30	8 −3	90 −20	72 −11
2.	88 −24	59 −38	43 −31	50 −40	48 −17	72 −62
3.	25 −15	94 − 4	50 −30	35 − 3	27 −10	13 −12
4.	53 −40	14 − 3	18 −10	55 −42	9 −2	10 − 8
5.	49 −18	74 − 3	59 −27	68 − 7	93 −22	38 −37
6.	79 −35	21 −11	46 −42	78 −64	15 − 4	87 −35
7.	25 −13	71 −20	46 −23	56 −41	85 −63	99 −77

Lesson 1.3 Adding Three or More Numbers (single digit)

$$\begin{array}{c} 2 \\ 6 \\ +7 \end{array} \searrow \quad \begin{array}{c} \\ 8 \\ +\ 7 \\ \hline 1\ 5 \end{array}$$

$$\begin{array}{c} 3 \\ 4 \\ 7 \\ +1 \end{array} \searrow \begin{array}{c} \\ \\ 7 \\ +1 \end{array} \rightarrow \begin{array}{c} 7 \\ 7 \\ +1 \end{array} \searrow \begin{array}{c} \\ 14 \\ +\ 1 \\ \hline 1\ 5 \end{array}$$

Add.

	a	b	c	d	e	f	g	h
1.	3 4 +5	2 6 +3	7 5 +3	6 3 +7	8 7 +2	9 8 +1	3 6 +8	1 7 +6
2.	4 6 +8	3 5 +2	1 5 +7	8 5 +3	4 7 +8	3 8 +9	2 6 +9	3 3 +7
3.	8 7 +5	8 3 +5	3 8 +2	2 8 +6	6 7 +8	3 6 +9	1 8 +7	5 7 +9
4.	1 3 5 +7	2 6 7 +4	1 5 9 +7	3 5 4 +6	2 2 2 +8	1 7 8 +9	4 4 5 +6	3 4 6 +8
5.	2 6 4 +8	2 2 8 +7	4 5 7 +9	3 3 4 +4	5 5 4 +3	6 3 7 +1	5 4 8 +9	1 7 1 +9
6.	9 1 7 +2	3 4 7 +8	2 5 7 +4	5 3 6 +5	8 3 9 +2	4 6 8 +3	7 3 7 +3	2 1 8 +5

Lesson 1.4 Adding through 2 Digits (with renaming)

	Add the ones.	Add the tens.

$$
\begin{array}{r} 52 \\ +29 \\ \hline \end{array}
$$

$$2 + 9 = 11 \text{ or } 10 + 1 \longrightarrow 1$$

$$
\begin{array}{r} {\scriptstyle 1} \\ 52 \\ +29 \\ \hline 1 \end{array}
$$

$$
\begin{array}{r} {\scriptstyle 1} \\ 52 \quad \text{addend} \\ +29 \quad \text{addend} \\ \hline 81 \quad \text{sum} \end{array}
$$

Add.

	a	b	c	d	e	f
1.	36 +15	29 +18	57 +23	18 +13	74 + 6	8 +27
2.	88 + 3	47 +17	27 +47	55 +26	19 +15	51 +19
3.	65 +26	39 +39	25 +25	45 +45	36 +48	75 +16
4.	37 +26	14 +48	13 +68	48 +22	37 +17	72 +18
5.	65 +25	9 +48	7 +77	82 + 9	28 + 9	48 +32
6.	39 +29	28 +28	29 + 9	28 +57	19 +14	9 +72
7.	75 + 7	73 + 9	36 +36	78 +18	19 +19	43 +17

Lesson 1.5 Adding Three or More Numbers (2 digit)

	Add the ones.	Add the tens.

```
addend ——→    26
addend ——→    38
addend ——→  +56
         ———————
6 + 8 + 6 = 20    20 = 20 + 0
```

Add the ones.
```
      2
     26
     38
   +56
   ————
      0
```

Add the tens.
```
   2
  26  ←— addend
  38  ←— addend
+ 56  ←— addend
 ————
 120  ←— sum
```

20 + 20 + 30 + 50 = 120   120 = 100 + 20

Add.

	a	b	c	d	e	f
1.	27 32 +43	39 48 +76	48 68 +78	97 85 +63	45 74 +48	97 23 +19
2.	77 99 +32	81 19 +38	53 78 +89	75 69 +78	38 57 +75	92 89 +95
3.	37 29 +49	87 78 +95	38 49 +57	42 28 +66	56 65 +77	19 37 +49
4.	35 73 57 +66	73 28 40 +66	88 22 38 +82	75 24 93 +51	29 93 37 +55	21 62 45 +38
5.	51 71 89 +99	20 18 39 +47	17 45 83 +97	27 58 74 +63	13 39 57 +89	57 33 71 +66
6.	39 29 58 +78	13 25 77 +89	27 53 68 +74	27 48 31 +97	22 17 39 +45	39 49 66 +77

Name _____

Lesson 1.6 Subtracting 2 Digits from 3 Digits (with renaming)

To subtract the ones, rename 5 tens and 3 ones as "4 tens and 13 ones."

	Subtract the ones.	Subtract the tens.	Subtract the hundreds.

minuend → 1 5 3   1 5̶ 3̶⁴¹³   1 5̶ 3̶⁴¹³   1 5̶ 3̶⁴¹³   1 5̶ 3̶⁴¹³
subtrahend → − 3 7   − 3 7   − 3 7   − 3 7   − 3 7
difference →   6   1 6   1 1 6

Subtract.

	a	b	c	d	e	f
1.	175 − 38	132 − 17	175 − 56	134 − 29	144 − 28	156 − 38
2.	182 − 73	177 − 59	123 − 18	141 − 33	173 − 54	182 − 48
3.	141 − 29	193 − 47	165 − 46	152 − 37	172 − 29	161 − 27
4.	183 − 68	127 − 18	134 − 19	172 − 57	124 − 17	153 − 37
5.	171 − 39	146 − 27	183 − 68	191 − 72	173 − 47	157 − 38
6.	128 − 19	172 − 36	156 − 29	177 − 39	152 − 19	174 − 38
7.	145 − 26	161 − 33	173 − 37	127 − 18	153 − 28	191 − 73

Lesson 1.6 Subtracting 2 Digits from 3 Digits
(with renaming)

Rename 515 as "5 hundreds, 0 tens, and 15 ones." Subtract the ones.	Then, rename "4 hundreds, 10 tens, and 15 ones." Subtract the tens.	Subtract the hundreds.

$$\begin{array}{r} 5\,1\,5 \\ -\ \ 2\,7 \\ \hline \end{array}$$

$$\begin{array}{r} {}^{0\ 15}5\,\cancel{1}\,\cancel{5} \\ -\ \ 2\,7 \\ \hline 8 \end{array}$$

$$\begin{array}{r} {}^{4\ 10\ 15}\cancel{5}\,\cancel{1}\,\cancel{5} \\ -\ \ 2\,7 \\ \hline 8\,8 \end{array}$$

$$\begin{array}{r} {}^{4\ 10\ 15}\cancel{5}\,\cancel{1}\,\cancel{5} \\ -\ \ 2\,7 \\ \hline 4\,8\,8 \end{array}$$ ← minuend
← subtrahend
← difference

Subtract.

	a	b	c	d	e	f
1.	138 − 59	162 − 79	155 − 66	128 − 59	147 − 58	174 − 85
2.	131 − 49	153 − 67	167 − 79	144 − 58	172 − 89	125 − 38
3.	114 − 37	134 − 56	181 − 92	133 − 44	127 − 49	174 − 88
4.	122 − 88	154 − 77	161 − 94	166 − 87	127 − 58	172 − 99
5.	177 − 88	123 − 45	147 − 68	181 − 95	175 − 89	141 − 83
6.	185 − 97	173 − 87	142 − 84	177 − 98	136 − 49	123 − 77
7.	127 − 58	126 − 78	166 − 89	137 − 88	153 − 84	175 − 97

Lesson 1.7 Thinking Subtraction for Addition

These numbers should be the same.

$$\begin{array}{r} 55 \\ +43 \\ \hline 98 \\ -43 \\ \hline 55 \end{array}$$

To check
55 + 43 = 98,
subtract 43 from 98.

Add. Then, check your answer.

	a	b	c	d	e	f
1.	$\begin{array}{r}32\\+47\\\hline\\-\\\hline\end{array}$	$\begin{array}{r}63\\+19\\\hline\\-\\\hline\end{array}$	$\begin{array}{r}38\\+24\\\hline\\-\\\hline\end{array}$	$\begin{array}{r}52\\+47\\\hline\\-\\\hline\end{array}$	$\begin{array}{r}28\\+15\\\hline\\-\\\hline\end{array}$	$\begin{array}{r}75\\+15\\\hline\\-\\\hline\end{array}$
2.	$\begin{array}{r}48\\+27\\\hline\\-\\\hline\end{array}$	$\begin{array}{r}82\\+10\\\hline\\-\\\hline\end{array}$	$\begin{array}{r}56\\+38\\\hline\\-\\\hline\end{array}$	$\begin{array}{r}44\\+27\\\hline\\-\\\hline\end{array}$	$\begin{array}{r}28\\+27\\\hline\\-\\\hline\end{array}$	$\begin{array}{r}39\\+32\\\hline\\-\\\hline\end{array}$
3.	$\begin{array}{r}31\\+59\\\hline\\-\\\hline\end{array}$	$\begin{array}{r}43\\+18\\\hline\\-\\\hline\end{array}$	$\begin{array}{r}61\\+29\\\hline\\-\\\hline\end{array}$	$\begin{array}{r}125\\+\ 17\\\hline\\-\\\hline\end{array}$	$\begin{array}{r}155\\+\ 38\\\hline\\-\\\hline\end{array}$	$\begin{array}{r}205\\+\ 69\\\hline\\-\\\hline\end{array}$
4.	$\begin{array}{r}199\\+\ 14\\\hline\\-\\\hline\end{array}$	$\begin{array}{r}128\\+\ 33\\\hline\\-\\\hline\end{array}$	$\begin{array}{r}125\\+\ 50\\\hline\\-\\\hline\end{array}$	$\begin{array}{r}109\\+\ 32\\\hline\\-\\\hline\end{array}$	$\begin{array}{r}155\\+\ 27\\\hline\\-\\\hline\end{array}$	$\begin{array}{r}137\\+\ 29\\\hline\\-\\\hline\end{array}$

Lesson 1.8 Thinking Addition for Subtraction

These numbers should be the same.

$$
\begin{array}{r}
138 \\
-24 \\
\hline
114 \\
+24 \\
\hline
138
\end{array}
$$

To check
138 − 24 = 114,
add 24 to 114.

Subtract. Then, check your answer.

	a	b	c	d	e	f

1.

$$
\begin{array}{r} 88 \\ -45 \\ \hline \end{array}
\qquad
\begin{array}{r} 23 \\ -19 \\ \hline \end{array}
\qquad
\begin{array}{r} 47 \\ -28 \\ \hline \end{array}
\qquad
\begin{array}{r} 95 \\ -38 \\ \hline \end{array}
\qquad
\begin{array}{r} 74 \\ -27 \\ \hline \end{array}
\qquad
\begin{array}{r} 98 \\ -73 \\ \hline \end{array}
$$

+ _____   + _____   + _____   + _____   + _____   + _____

2.

$$
\begin{array}{r} 38 \\ -17 \\ \hline \end{array}
\qquad
\begin{array}{r} 68 \\ -27 \\ \hline \end{array}
\qquad
\begin{array}{r} 54 \\ -36 \\ \hline \end{array}
\qquad
\begin{array}{r} 49 \\ -32 \\ \hline \end{array}
\qquad
\begin{array}{r} 29 \\ -10 \\ \hline \end{array}
\qquad
\begin{array}{r} 78 \\ -39 \\ \hline \end{array}
$$

+ _____   + _____   + _____   + _____   + _____   + _____

3.

$$
\begin{array}{r} 155 \\ -28 \\ \hline \end{array}
\qquad
\begin{array}{r} 132 \\ -38 \\ \hline \end{array}
\qquad
\begin{array}{r} 179 \\ -82 \\ \hline \end{array}
\qquad
\begin{array}{r} 127 \\ -89 \\ \hline \end{array}
\qquad
\begin{array}{r} 141 \\ -62 \\ \hline \end{array}
\qquad
\begin{array}{r} 137 \\ -52 \\ \hline \end{array}
$$

+ _____   + _____   + _____   + _____   + _____   + _____

4.

$$
\begin{array}{r} 187 \\ -99 \\ \hline \end{array}
\qquad
\begin{array}{r} 119 \\ -20 \\ \hline \end{array}
\qquad
\begin{array}{r} 192 \\ -73 \\ \hline \end{array}
\qquad
\begin{array}{r} 108 \\ -39 \\ \hline \end{array}
\qquad
\begin{array}{r} 188 \\ -90 \\ \hline \end{array}
\qquad
\begin{array}{r} 164 \\ -78 \\ \hline \end{array}
$$

+ _____   + _____   + _____   + _____   + _____   + _____

Lesson 1.9 Problem Solving

Solve each problem.

1. Isabel Jones needs to sell 175 calendars to raise money for the school band. She already sold 89 calendars. How many more calendars does she have to sell?

   She has to sell _____ calendars.

   1.

2. Jacob Elementary School had a book drive. On Monday, the students collected 95 books. They collected 78 more books on Tuesday. How many books did the students collect?

   The students collected _____ books.

   2.

3. The Grover family went on a spring vacation. Their cabin is 305 miles away. If they drive 98 miles the first day, how many more miles do they have to drive to get to the cabin?

   They must drive _____ more miles.

   3.

4. The school cafeteria had an all-you-can-eat pizza party for the entire school. They made 215 slices of cheese pizza and 120 slices of pepperoni pizza. How many slices of pizza did they make?

   They made _____ slices of pizza.

   4.

5. There are 250 species of turtles and tortoises in the world. If there are 86 species listed as endangered, how many species of turtles and tortoises are not endangered?

   There are _____ species of turtles and tortoises that are not endangered.

   5.

Check What You Learned

Adding and Subtracting 1 and 2 Digits

Add or subtract.

	a	b	c	d	e	f
1.	43 +27	57 +21	37 +15	73 +28	256 + 43	75 +25
2.	13 10 + 8	27 5 +23	238 + 68	91 82 +73	105 92 + 14	156 + 48
3.	21 +13	253 + 42	137 + 28	79 +97	103 + 18	65 +17
4.	73 21 +10	432 + 48	14 18 +32	66 +34	34 45 +57	13 +74
5.	77 +15	104 + 76	90 +45	143 + 38	103 + 97	91 +17
6.	245 − 32	105 − 16	35 −12	72 −28	91 −73	35 − 7
7.	107 − 34	94 −25	215 − 26	88 −49	173 − 28	72 −61
8.	35 −16	108 − 19	51 −32	125 − 15	199 − 84	84 −26
9.	147 − 48	62 −22	57 −32	111 − 12	123 − 48	92 −29
10.	187 − 38	55 −18	110 − 32	36 −17	192 − 83	44 −25

Check What You Learned

SHOW YOUR WORK

Adding and Subtracting 1 and 2 Digits

Solve each problem.

11. Tonya and her friends are collecting cans to recycle. Tonya has 55 cans, Irene has 32 cans, and Heather has 13 cans. How many cans do they have altogether?

They have _____ cans.

11.

12. The Liberty football team is raising money for its new uniforms by running a car wash. They need to wash 210 cars to raise all the money. If they have washed 98 cars already, how many more cars do they need to wash?

They need to wash _____ more cars.

12.

13. Ms. Yolanda Brooks' science class is studying the environment around the school. The boys in the class counted 57 different plants and the girls counted 25 different types of animals. How many plants and animals did the class find altogether?

The class found _____ plants and animals.

13.

14. On a field trip, two sisters found frog eggs in a pond. Desiree found 82 eggs and Shanee found 118 eggs. How many frog eggs did the sisters find?

They found _____ frog eggs.

14.

15. At the bake sale, students brought in 115 different types of cupcakes, 95 types of brownies, and 85 types of cookies. How many different types of baked goods did the students bring in?

They brought in _____ different types of baked goods.

15.

Check What You Know

Numeration through 1,000,000

Write each number in expanded form.

	a	b	c
1.	3,245	973	51
	_____	_____	_____
2.	6,675	845,450	790
	_____	_____	_____

What digit is in the place named?

	a	b
3.	945	4,332
	tens	hundreds
	_____ is in the tens place.	_____ is in the hundreds place.
4.	52,321	528,455
	thousands	ones
	_____ is in the thousands place.	_____ is in the ones place.
5.	495,362	9,365,732
	ten thousands	millions
	_____ is in the ten thousands place.	_____ is in the millions place.

Compare each pair of numbers. Write >, <, or =.

	a	b	c
6.	4,312 __ 4,213	95 __ 58	408 __ 480
7.	52,650 __ 52,560	610 __ 672	72 __ 62
8.	52,173 __ 520,173	4,675,321 __ 4,751,670	25 __ 52
9.	158,325 __ 158,325	652 __ 256	8,910,003 __ 8,910,003

Check What You Know

Numeration through 1,000,000

Round each number to the place named.

	a	b	c
10.	7,649 thousands	932 hundreds	553,972 hundred thousands
	_____	_____	_____
11.	9,732,005 millions	75 tens	1,675 hundreds
	_____	_____	_____
12.	82,397 ten thousands	928 tens	682,349 thousands
	_____	_____	_____

Show the value of the 9 in each number.

	a	b	c	d
13.	95,235	479	1,976,235	5,392
	_____	_____	_____	_____
14.	9,003,452	2,349,003	5,009,321	8,793,215
	_____	_____	_____	_____
15.	6,000,942	3,209	794,367	9,003,400
	_____	_____	_____	_____

Lesson 2.1 Understanding Place Value (to hundreds)

Write each number in expanded form.

	a	b	c	d
1.	54	608	32	421
	50+4			
2.	430	549	75	699
3.	one hundred thirty-two	seven hundred twenty-one	thirty-nine	eighty-seven
4.	nine hundred eleven	five hundred thirteen	one hundred ninety	seventy

Write the numerical value of the digit in the place named.

	a	b	c	d
5.	872 tens	934 hundreds	326 ones	304 ones
	70			
6.	799 hundreds	663 tens	309 tens	995 hundreds

Name the place of the underlined digit.

	a	b
7.	85,0̲34	9,4̲32
	_____ is in the _____ place.	_____ is in the _____ place.
8.	11,987̲	75,34̲2
	_____ is in the _____ place.	_____ is in the _____ place.

Lesson 2.2 Understanding Place Value (to ten thousands)

Write each number in expanded form.

	a	b	c
1.	3,465	25,639	43,645
	3,000 + 400 + 60 + 5	_____	_____
2.	twenty-four thousand	sixty-nine thousand three	90,327
	_____	_____	_____
3.	fifty-two thousand three hundred four	65,792	4,009
	_____	_____	_____

Name the place of the underlined digit.

	a	b
4.	7̲3,654	9,3̲21
	_____ is in the _____ place.	_____ is in the _____ place.
5.	39̲,524	65,5̲66
	_____ is in the _____ place.	_____ is in the _____ place.
6.	7̲9,984	85,231̲
	_____ is in the _____ place.	_____ is in the _____ place.

Write the numerical value of the digit in the place named.

	a	b	c
7.	56,432 ten thousands	7,236 thousands	64,785 hundreds
	50,000	_____	_____
8.	5,699 tens	65,981 ten thousands	93,492 thousands
	_____	_____	_____

Lesson 2.3 Understanding Place Value
(to hundred thousands)

Name the place of the underlined digit.

	a	**b**
1.	1<u>5</u>2,731	<u>2</u>93,768
	_____ is in the _____ place.	_____ is in the _____ place.
2.	985,<u>6</u>85	<u>5</u>56,665
	_____ is in the _____ place.	_____ is in the _____ place.

Which digit is in the place named?

3.	50,975 ten thousands	986,580 hundred thousands
	_____	_____
4.	179,802 thousands	506,671 ten thousands
	_____	_____
5.	865,003 ten thousands	997,780 hundred thousands
	_____	_____

Write each number in expanded form.

6.	653,410	76,982
	_____	_____
7.	sixty-two thousand five hundred twelve	103,254
	_____	_____
8.	199,482	32,451
	_____	_____

Lesson 2.4 Understanding Place Value (to millions)

Write the numerical value of the digit in the place named.

	a	b	c	d
I.	5,363,246 millions	952,418 ten thousands	4,510,367 tens	8,123,405 ones
	5,000,000	5	6	5
2.	9,867,823 hundred thousands	567,345 thousands	1,328,976 millions	5,004,002 thousands
	8	7	1	4

Write each number in expanded form.

	a	b
3.	two million five hundred thousand fifty-five	513,468
	2,000,000+50+50,000	57,000
4.	598,721	9,342,751
5.	three hundred seventy-one thousand eighty-eight	81,203

Name the place of the underlined digit.

6. 2,5̲63,740   3̲,297,134

_____ is in the _____ place   _____ is in the _____ place

7. 8,76̲1,089   9̲,345,187

_____ is in the _____ place   _____ is in the _____ place

8. 8̲59,632   4̲,689,322

_____ is in the _____ place   _____ is in the _____ place

Lesson 2.5 Rounding

Round 15,897 to the nearest thousand. Look at the hundreds digit. 15,<u>8</u>97	Round 234,054 to the nearest hundred. Look at the tens digit. 234,0<u>5</u>4
8 is greater than or equal to 5, so round 5 to 6 in the thousands place. Follow with zeros.	5 is greater than or equal to 5, so round 0 to 1 in the hundreds place. Follow with zeros.
16,000	234,100

Round to the nearest ten.

	a	b	c	d	e	f
1.	6,421	5,882	45,288	975	13,936	842
2.	9,855	26,917	984	95,645	8,673	29,981

Round to the nearest hundred.

3.	325,793	49,832	123,652	24,635	199,794	79,342
4.	798,759	58,345	9,873	8,375	10,097	1,987,654

Round to the nearest thousand.

5.	567,523	93,567	4,378	12,499	747,399	9,385
6.	987,436	346,436	98,345	8,564	75,459	187,349

Lesson 2.5   Rounding

Round 783,538 to the nearest ten thousand. | Round 2,895,321 to the nearest million.
Look at the thousands digit. 78<u>3</u>,538 | Look at the hundred thousands digit.
2,<u>8</u>95,321

3 is less than 5, so keep 8 in the ten | 8 is greater than or equal to 5, so round 2
thousands place. Follow with zeros. | to 3 in the millions place. Follow with zeros.

780,000 | 3,000,000

Round to the nearest ten thousand.

	a	b	c	d	e
1.	726,034	1,456,203	735,976	5,546,937	49,324
2.	184,564	7,735,567	34,596	476,435	5,638,748

Round to the nearest hundred thousand.

3.	4,835,694	354,543	9,325,987	7,952,436	456,987
4.	8,745,123	1,057,251	435,900	9,730,204	576,132

Round to the nearest million.

5.	7,499,887	6,576,362	2,245,984	4,458,876	7,561,110
6.	1,935,761	3,666,345	7,468,994	5,565,740	8,089,768

Lesson 2.6 Greater Than, Less Than, or Equal To

Inequalities are statements in which the numbers are not equal.

Compare 35 and 42.
35 $\leq$ 42

Compare the values.
Look at the tens.
3 tens is less than 4 tens.
35 is less than 42.
This is an inequality.

< means "is less than."
> means "is greater than."
= means "is equal to."

Compare 110 and 112.
110 $\leq$ 112

Compare the values.
Since the hundreds and tens are equal, look at the ones.
110 is less than 112.
This is an inequality.

Compare 55 to 55.
55 $=$ 55

These numbers are equal, so this is not an inequality.

Compare each pair of numbers. Write >, <, or =.

	a	b	c
1.	105 __ 120	52 __ 35	10,362 __ 10,562
2.	5,002 __ 2,113	713 __ 731	12,317 __ 11,713
3.	115,000 __ 105,000	23 __ 32	142 __ 142
4.	310 __ 290	715 __ 725	1,132,700 __ 1,032,700
5.	616 __ 106	119,000 __ 120,000	48,112 __ 48,212
6.	823 __ 821	2,003,461 __ 2,004,461	7,903 __ 9,309
7.	30 __ 25	47,999 __ 45,999	19,900 __ 19,090
8.	111 __ 111	386,712 __ 386,711	615 __ 614

Lesson 2.6 Greater Than, Less Than, or Equal To

Compare the numbers. Write <, >, or =.

This statement is called an **inequality** because the two numbers are not equal.

4,326 _>_ 4,226

Look at the hundreds. 3 hundreds is greater than 2 hundreds.

Compare each pair of numbers. Write >, <, or =.

	a	b	c
1.	3,647 __ 36,647	4,678 __ 4,768	68,035 __ 68,025
2.	4,102,364 __ 4,201,364	56,703 __ 56,702	125,125 __ 125,150
3.	90,368 __ 90,369	5,654,308 __ 5,546,309	65,003 __ 65,013
4.	4,567,801 __ 456,780	7,621 __ 7,261	769,348 __ 759,348
5.	506,708 __ 506,807	1,365,333 __ 1,365,333	9,982 __ 9,928
6.	224,364 __ 234,364	32,506 __ 23,605	7,850 __ 7,850
7.	3,204,506 __ 3,204,606	9,851 __ 9,850	2,000,567 __ 2,001,567
8.	430,632 __ 480,362	49,984 __ 49,984	5,640,002 __ 5,639,992
9.	172,302 __ 173,302	212,304 __ 212,304	6,886 __ 6,896

Check What You Learned

Numeration through 1,000,000

Write each number in expanded form.

	a	b
1.	1,965,012	693,145
2.	103,458	23,972
3.	471,440	18,321
4.	98,485	313,082

Name the value of the place named.

	a	b	c	d
5.	1,235,012 thousands	546,102 tens	1,141 hundreds	499,612 tens
6.	743,218 ten thousands	821,812 hundred thousands	567,982 tens	8,762 thousands
7.	3,210,456 millions	589,123 hundred thousands	1,934,763 tens	37,103 ones

Check What You Learned

Numeration through 1,000,000

Round each number to the nearest ten thousand.

	a	b	c	d	e
8.	2,396,473	763,465	85,123	2,391,362	625,104
9.	305,419	8,939,721	434,599	49,002	2,009,452

Round each number to the nearest hundred thousand.

10.	2,952,430	783,210	3,085,997	876,520	385,921
11.	509,815	7,651,298	198,205	6,519,190	457,213

Round each number to the nearest million.

12.	2,456,997	9,352,697	6,976,542	4,561,004	7,395,467
13.	1,596,412	7,396,732	9,235,987	3,396,374	5,564,320

Compare each pair of numbers. Write >, <, or =.

	a	b	c
14.	24,124 __ 24,224	1,975,212 __ 1,985,212	56,410 __ 54,408
15.	509,712 __ 590,172	2,341,782 __ 2,341,782	976,152 __ 967,932
16.	6,918 __ 6,818	49,917 __ 49,907	3,425,556 __ 3,524,565
17.	8,724,100 __ 5,724,101	3,002,019 __ 3,002,109	2,418 __ 2,418

Check What You Know

Adding and Subtracting 3 through 5 Digits

Add.

	a	b	c	d	e
1.	562 +217	1452 + 519	732 +195	3721 + 146	5605 +1324
2.	4003 +1717	193 +117	2281 +1307	624 +624	1502 + 375
3.	443 +237	5127 + 310	6152 +1343	9730 + 169	1070 + 910
4.	3489 +1301	2811 +1187	6423 + 314	900 +134	3007 +2993

Subtract.

	a	b	c	d	e
5.	2817 − 314	987 −445	7760 −1352	583 −472	9057 −3152
6.	8648 − 526	9382 −7481	5533 −4622	7520 −1418	4103 − 136
7.	5799 −3182	2872 − 591	1890 − 727	2378 −1060	22486 − 475
8.	972 −175	7003 −1762	834 −514	71487 − 2271	9772 − 379

Check What You Know

Adding and Subtracting 3 through 5 Digits

Solve each problem.

9. Pablo and his family love to travel. This summer, they traveled 2,433 miles to visit relatives. If Pablo's family traveled 1,561 miles last year, how many miles have they traveled in the past two years?

They traveled _____ miles in the past two years.

9.

10. The Brown County Humane Society took in 15,538 pets in the first six months of the year. The rest of the year, they took in 10,456 pets. How many pets did they take in during the year?

They took in _____ pets during the year.

10.

11. Springfield School District bought 578 new science books. There are 1,976 students in the science classes. How many students will not receive a new book?

There will be _____ students without a new book.

11.

12. Yoki visited the United States for the first time. He had to ride a bus for 1,472 miles to get to Ashland City. The bus broke down after 1,227 miles. How many more miles did Yoki have to travel?

He had _____ miles left to travel.

12.

13. Trey is getting ready to go to basketball camp. There are 213 players arriving on Friday and 131 players arriving on Saturday. If Trey arrives on Sunday with 104 more players, how many players will be at the camp?

There will be _____ players at the camp.

13.

Lesson 3.1 Adding 3-Digit Numbers

Add the ones.	Add the tens.	Add the hundreds.
256	$\overset{1}{2}$56	$\overset{1}{2}$56 ⟵ addend
+253	+253	+253 ⟵ addend
$\underline{9}$	$\underline{0}$9	$\underline{5}$09 ⟵ sum

Add.

	a	b	c	d	e	f
1.	727 +182	503 +247	482 +107	132 +127	663 +125	823 +170
2.	337 +224	281 +127	407 +313	557 +223	487 +111	723 +432
3.	804 +179	198 +198	374 +298	503 +307	413 +344	723 +177
4.	652 +328	298 +133	511 +347	734 +536	309 +403	178 +131
5.	733 +156	543 +123	317 +226	199 +188	904 +396	825 +125
6.	902 +112	284 +173	610 +330	448 +136	709 +148	138 +125
7.	700 +493	509 +409	822 +188	294 +103	956 +143	248 +109

Lesson 3.2 Subtracting through 4 Digits

Subtract the ones.	Rename and subtract the tens.	Rename and subtract the hundreds.

$$\begin{array}{r}1748\\-952\\\hline 6\end{array}$$

$$\begin{array}{r}\overset{6\ 14}{1\cancel{7}\cancel{4}8}\\-952\\\hline 96\end{array}$$

$$\begin{array}{r}\overset{16}{\overset{6\ 14}{\cancel{1}\cancel{7}\cancel{4}8}}\longleftarrow\text{minuend}\\-952\longleftarrow\text{subtrahend}\\\hline 796\longleftarrow\text{difference}\end{array}$$

Subtract.

	a	b	c	d	e	f
1.	3621 −2710	947 −338	1479 − 346	403 −172	5521 − 725	800 −401
2.	5347 − 849	1763 −1452	937 −647	6633 −3366	710 −607	4036 −2072
3.	2786 −1684	475 −285	7036 − 936	888 −364	1010 − 909	1505 − 436
4.	8287 − 475	432 −151	4675 −3765	1403 − 647	872 −721	6483 −4894
5.	2440 −2332	5280 −2502	5420 −1938	992 −367	5678 −1234	3146 − 454
6.	2535 −2312	4311 − 564	7653 −1953	1992 − 741	5244 −2631	7198 −2112

Lesson 3.3 Adding 4-Digit Numbers

Add the ones.	Add the tens.	Add the hundreds.	Add the thousands.
1 5 6 4	1 5 6 4	1 5 6 4	1 5 6 4 ←—— addend
+4 3 2 2	+4 3 2 2	+4 3 2 2	+4 3 2 2 ←—— addend
6	8 6	8 8 6	5 8 8 6 ←—— sum

Add.

	a	b	c	d	e
1.	1576 +1321	4009 +1019	2806 +1404	7314 +3728	6410 +2302
2.	3309 +2190	5754 +3475	5732 +4260	2895 +1435	7311 +1695
3.	5094 +1557	3150 +1472	1949 +1799	2473 +1303	2487 +1658
4.	1887 +1884	2797 +2613	2005 +2023	7300 +1795	6114 +1876
5.	3113 +2002	1720 +2071	4025 +1883	5758 +3837	6754 +1006
6.	7430 +2670	3552 +4431	3020 +4070	1448 +1336	8467 +1452
7.	8970 +5732	1776 +1406	5123 +3011	2882 +1999	4909 +2080

Lesson 3.4 Problem Solving

Solve each problem.

1. A moving company moved 3,400 families this year. Last year, the company moved 2,549 families. How many families did the company move in the past two years?

   The company moved _____ families.

2. Buckton pet store buys a total of 7,307 crickets every month for lizard food. If the store needs 230 crickets per month to feed their own lizards, how many crickets are left to sell to customers?

   They have _____ crickets left to sell to customers.

3. James and Curtis entered into a rollerblade racing event. There were 121 people entered in the event and 240 people watching. How many people were there in all?

   There were _____ people at the event.

4. The football team at Franklin High weighed in at 2,150 pounds. The football team at Union High weighed in at 2,019 pounds. How much more did the Franklin High team weigh?

   The Franklin High team weighed _____ pounds more.

5. Southgate Nursery sold 561 flowers on Saturday and 359 flowers on Sunday. How many flowers did Southgate Nursery sell over the weekend?

   Southgate Nursery sold _____ flowers.

6. In one morning, workers picked two loads of corn from the fields. The first load weighed 1,558 pounds and the second load weighed 1,600 pounds. How many pounds of corn did the workers pick that morning?

   The workers picked _____ pounds of corn.

1.

2.

3.

4.

5.   **6.**

Lesson 3.5 Subtracting 4- and 5-Digit Numbers

Subtract the ones.	Subtract the tens.	Rename and subtract the hundreds.	Rename and subtract the thousands.

$$\begin{array}{r} 13546 \\ -7643 \\ \hline 3 \end{array}$$

$$\begin{array}{r} 13546 \\ -7643 \\ \hline 03 \end{array}$$

$$\begin{array}{r} {\scriptstyle 2\ 15} \\ 13\cancel{5}46 \\ -7643 \\ \hline 903 \end{array}$$

$$\begin{array}{r} {\scriptstyle 0\ 12\ 15} \\ \cancel{1}\cancel{3}\cancel{5}46 \\ -7643 \\ \hline 5903 \end{array}$$ ← minuend / subtrahend / difference

Subtract.

	a	b	c	d	e
1.	25625 − 6510	73461 − 3861	40305 − 6307	15898 − 4775	66859 −34437
2.	80247 −15136	33969 −20979	95348 − 6007	59109 −45207	82468 − 3547
3.	45244 −45227	63207 − 8009	77528 −68431	10826 − 2715	57578 −23888
4.	22127 − 3125	50003 −15102	85713 − 7649	27791 −13782	84875 −74046
5.	99818 −66919	39000 − 8007	19909 − 8723	29301 −15082	13109 −11008
6.	10806 − 6090	42875 −33705	30000 −15000	24080 −16427	16046 − 8204
7.	76115 −24007	87223 − 8224	24955 −13865	30080 − 2400	67660 −55084

Lesson 3.6 Adding 3 or More Numbers (through 4 digits)

Add each place value
from right to left.

$$
\begin{array}{r}
\overset{1\ 1}{3\,2\,5\,1} \\
3\,3\,5 \\
+\ \ 2\,4\,8 \\
\hline
3\,8\,3\,4
\end{array}
\qquad
\begin{array}{r}
\overset{1\ 1\ 1}{2\,4\,5\,6} \\
3\,2\,1\,0 \\
4\,1\,0 \\
+\ \ 2\,3\,5 \\
\hline
6\,3\,1\,1
\end{array}
$$

Add.

	a	b	c	d	e
1.	460	300	605	600	1324
	240	305	245	42	720
	16	240	113	36	310
	+ 14	+ 65	+105	+ 29	+ 209

2.	6410	812	7615	617	2012
	4205	16	1207	522	150
	+3112	+ 12	+1152	+113	+ 150

3.	1935	9132	5903	7213	942
	1690	7516	4051	4132	483
	130	1509	1230	3715	305
	+ 117	+ 123	+1005	+1503	+236

4.	5017	8800	1725	7525	4973
	1243	5008	1528	5150	2007
	+ 502	+4112	+1341	+1000	+1221

5.	3417	5009	4107	7010	5139
	2345	4103	3224	5528	4722
	1132	2705	1115	3175	1056
	+ 305	+1003	+ 607	+ 948	+1013

Lesson 3.7 Adding 4- and 5-Digit Numbers

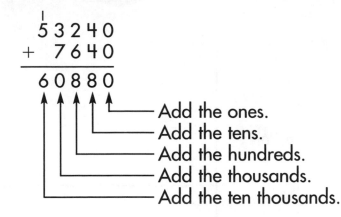

$$
\begin{array}{r}
{}^{1}\;5\,3\,2\,4\,0 \\
+\;\;7\,6\,4\,0 \\
\hline
6\,0\,8\,8\,0
\end{array}
$$

Add the ones.
Add the tens.
Add the hundreds.
Add the thousands.
Add the ten thousands.

$$
\begin{array}{r}
5\,3\,2\,4\,0 \longleftarrow \text{addend} \\
+\;\;7\,6\,4\,0 \longleftarrow \text{addend} \\
\hline
6\,0\,8\,8\,0 \longleftarrow \text{sum}
\end{array}
$$

Add.

	a	b	c	d	e
1.	4301 +7256	23125 + 1150	7372 +1727	74323 +28057	2248 +1184
2.	23703 + 6147	9100 +3498	13788 + 9093	5009 +5009	10735 + 5781
3.	5112 +3227	45173 + 3217	4880 +2009	25883 +24458	82048 + 8953
4.	10738 + 1327	8327 +2735	64576 +13610	7993 +6814	23230 +17075
5.	2376 +1484	33782 + 5118	9109 +4701	40119 +25118	7594 +3505
6.	14157 + 3352	5213 +3004	32705 +18805	2484 +1555	15978 +14605

Lesson 3.8   Problem Solving   **SHOW YOUR WORK**

Solve each problem.

1. Last year, 5,670 teenagers lived in Perry County. This year, 732 more teenagers moved there. If 2,115 more teenagers move in, how many teenagers will live in Perry County?

There will be _____ teenagers living in Perry County.

2. There are about 4,300 species of mammals in the world. There are about 9,000 species of birds. About how many mammals and birds are there in the world?

There are _____ species of mammals and birds.

3. Mi-Ling and Chet Ai are interested in the planets. They found out Saturn is about 74,566 miles wide and Earth is about 7,926 miles wide. How much wider is Saturn?

Saturn is _____ miles wider.

4. Over the weekend, the Midmark Theater sold 1,208 buckets of popcorn, 2,543 sodas, and 973 boxes of candy. How many food items did the theater sell?

The theater sold _____ food items.

5. At the state fair, the candy booth was very popular. It had a swimming pool filled with chocolate-covered peanuts and pretzels. There was a total of 97,635 pieces of candy in the pool. The pool had 56,784 chocolate-covered peanuts. How many pretzels were there?

There were _____ pretzels.

1.

2.

3.

4.   **5.**

Lesson 3.9　Addition and Subtraction Practice

Add.

	a	b	c	d	e
1.	39741 + 4372	75103 + 1789	34396 +33715	60056 +13051	9408 +2592
2.	1515 +1212	10763 + 9275	66804 +32198	2575 +1984	25788 +17875
3.	13362 +44202	45245 + 2163	74612 + 3400	45220 + 1399	4998 +3975
4.	371 +287	2513 727 + 236	937 +793	815 673 +295	7035 1293 + 713

Subtract.

	a	b	c	d	e
5.	5703 −2147	13817 − 7616	1215 − 130	36973 −19782	7113 −6327
6.	79342 − 7983	44500 −24712	6137 −4372	60704 −50913	9702 −7512
7.	8791 − 370	3487 −1807	55013 − 5907	47893 −45797	8119 − 795
8.	84003 −26174	19834 − 9796	39137 −25126	6655 −4837	7841 − 957

Lesson 3.10   Addition and Subtraction Practice

Add.

	a	b	c	d	e
1.	6418 527 + 318	1385 972 + 113	5759 2132 + 784	9107 6048 + 710	1248 1212 +1047
2.	998 +795	10007 + 9323	72457 +38718	6514 +3572	105 +103

Subtract.

3.	8080 −4092	79998 −37948	47973 − 9007	7013 −6912	8173 −7289
4.	18873 −12092	51135 − 2076	5117 −4108	1195 − 945	7495 −6816

Add or subtract.

5.	4405 + 758	66481 − 8675	4007 −3216	12489 + 7981	2817 − 250
6.	341 +298	17116 + 8713	97581 −85762	6245 +5345	15035 − 7335
7.	14809 −12734	28785 +13816	9248 −4517	5217 +5172	92408 − 8862
8.	4500 3217 +2518	87672 −69318	5218 735 + 613	6208 +1517	7185 5807 + 914

Lesson 3.11 Estimating Sums and Differences

Round each number to the highest place value the numbers have in common. Then, add from right to left.

$$7365 \longrightarrow 7000$$
$$+\underline{5}613 \longrightarrow + 6000$$
$$13000$$

Round each number to the highest place value the numbers have in common. Then, subtract from right to left.

$$2718 \longrightarrow 2700$$
$$- \underline{5}96 \longrightarrow - 600$$
$$2100$$

Estimate the sum.

	a	b	c	d	e
1.	52708 + 8102	7385 +6814	914 +896	45036 +32516	17852 +15185
2.	7452 +6324	29715 +12152	64593 + 4452	913 +570	5490 + 742
3.	3750 +2852	87563 +21785	3385 +2300	58852 +15123	48736 + 9512

Estimate the difference.

4.	25917 - 6432	7255 - 852	8915 -7520	10972 - 3105	73917 -25842
5.	33972 -32914	4504 - 914	55482 - 6510	8152 -7395	25782 -14692
6.	1995 - 739	25987 - 365	13913 - 472	68792 - 9113	722 -591

Lesson 3.11 Problem Solving

SHOW YOUR WORK

Round each number to the highest place value the numbers have in common. Then, estimate the sum or difference for each problem.

1. Roberto and Steve counted the pennies they have been saving for 5 years. Roberto has 52,781 pennies and Steve has 58,972 pennies. About how many pennies do they have together?

   They have about _____ pennies.

2. A baseball team gave away free hats to 10,917 fans. There were 13,786 people at the game. About how many fans did not get a free hat?

   About _____ fans did not get a free hat.

3. Mr. Chien's art class melted down broken crayons to make a wax figure. The morning class melted 7,325 pieces. The afternoon class melted 6,800 pieces. About how many pieces did the class melt?

   The class melted about _____ pieces.

4. There are 5,248 different types of insects in Sue's neighborhood. About 518 of those can be harmful to people. About how many insects cannot hurt Sue?

   About _____ insects cannot hurt Sue.

5. Jasmine and her brother counted their button collection. Jasmine counted about 5,213 buttons in all. Her brother counted 973 buttons that were blue. About how many buttons were not blue?

   About _____ buttons were not blue.

6. The post office delivered about 55,002 letters to pen pals in England this year. Last year, the post office delivered 49,000 letters. About how many more letters did the post office deliver this year?

   The post office delivered about _____ more letters this year.

1.

2.

3.

4.

5.

6.

Check What You Learned

Adding and Subtracting 3 through 5 Digits

Add or subtract.

	a	b	c	d	e
1.	89700 +9313	49713 +13169	790 +304	1825 + 775	7914 + 308
2.	15431 +10917	50012 + 1597	2118 + 825	7381 +5964	52005 + 8007
3.	735 162 + 94	6280 +3770	2515 1003 + 714	68810 +43057	8291 6104 +5596
4.	68045 − 7210	3815 −2756	22816 −18792	7892 − 993	68613 −40007
5.	66891 − 9073	99895 −75872	7001 6342	9723 − 714	26819 − 7910
6.	2519 −1943	1050 − 713	70462 −70210	51372 − 8619	38982 −17551

Estimate the sum or difference.

	a	b	c	d	e
7.	52873 + 3219	4872 +1356	80972 + 7321	7298 + 753	48932 +30942
8.	4962 − 519	59782 −53973	87752 − 8521	7495 −6581	9325 −2513

Check What You Learned

SHOW YOUR WORK

Adding and Subtracting 3 through 5 Digits

Solve each problem.

9. Reva's doctor wants her to walk more for exercise. She has to walk 10,000 steps daily. On Saturday, she only walked 8,972 steps. How many more steps did Reva need to walk?

She needed to walk _____ more steps.

9.

10. Curtis wanted to paint his bedroom either blue or green. At the paint store, there were 785 shades of blue and 685 shades of green. How many color choices did Curtis have?

Curtis had _____ color choices.

10.

11. Clare collects stamps from around the world. She has 2,315 stamps so far, but her goal is to have 5,500 stamps. How many more stamps does she need to complete her collection?

She needs _____ more stamps.

11.

Round each number to the highest place value the numbers have in common. Then, estimate the sum or difference for each problem.

12. John's brother is in high school and needs to write a 1,500 word report on pollution. He has 842 words in the report so far. About how many more words does he need?

He needs about _____ more words.

12.

13. The hospital's service elevator can hold 12,560 pounds. A technician and equipment weigh 752 pounds. About how much more weight can the elevator hold?

The elevator can hold about _____ more pounds.

13.

Check What You Know

Multiplying through 3 Digits by 2 Digits

Multiply.

	a	b	c	d	e	f
1.	7 ×8	25 × 3	302 × 13	17 ×15	10 × 9	12 ×12
2.	315 × 47	9 ×9	91 ×52	32 ×33	403 × 7	93 × 8
3.	605 × 40	79 ×21	100 × 22	4 ×8	117 × 23	49 × 8
4.	750 × 23	10 ×10	794 × 2	75 ×25	11 ×11	972 × 3
5.	452 × 92	88 ×22	7 ×6	66 × 7	78 ×73	802 × 16
6.	872 × 21	33 ×70	8 ×8	109 × 42	618 × 47	500 × 30
7.	102 × 30	544 × 8	891 × 29	792 × 36	107 × 5	19 ×13
8.	618 × 12	748 × 5	89 ×60	72 × 5	118 × 37	500 × 90

Check What You Know

SHOW YOUR WORK

Multiplying through 3 Digits by 2 Digits

Solve each problem.

9. Students set up the chairs for the spring concert at Bethel High School. There were 25 rows with 10 chairs in each row. How many chairs did they set up?

They set up _____ chairs.

9.

10. The school carnival was a success. The school sold 99 tickets and each ticket was good for 2 rides. How many rides did the school sell?

The school sold _____ rides.

10.

11. At the Bead Shop, there are 25 rows of glass beads. If there are 320 glass beads in each row, how many glass beads are in the shop?

There are _____ glass beads in the shop.

11.

12. The cafeteria planned to bake 3 chocolate chip cookies for every student in the school. If there are 715 students, how many cookies does the cafeteria need to bake?

The cafeteria needs to bake _____ cookies.

12.

13. Crystal and Eva have been working 10 hours every week on their oral report on Rosa Parks. If they work on the report for 5 weeks, how many hours will they work on the report?

They will work _____ hours on the report.

13.

Lesson 4.1 Multiplying Single Digits

factor $\longrightarrow$ 7 $\longrightarrow$ Find the **7**-column.

factor $\longrightarrow \times$ 3 $\longrightarrow$ Find the **3**-row.

product $\longrightarrow$ 21 $\longrightarrow$ The product is named where the 7-column and the 3-row meet.

7-column

x	0	1	2	3	4	5	6	7	8	9
0	0	0	0	0	0	0	0	0	0	0
1	0	1	2	3	4	5	6	7	8	9
2	0	2	4	6	8	10	12	14	16	18
3	0	3	6	9	12	15	18	21	24	27
4	0	4	8	12	16	20	24	28	32	36
5	0	5	10	15	20	25	30	35	40	45
6	0	6	12	18	24	30	36	42	48	54
7	0	7	14	21	28	35	42	49	56	63
8	0	8	16	24	32	40	48	56	64	72
9	0	9	18	27	36	45	54	63	72	81

3-row

Use the table to multiply.

Multiply.

	a	b	c	d	e	f	g	h
1.	3 ×3	8 ×7	2 ×9	7 ×5	9 ×4	6 ×6	7 ×1	9 ×0
2.	9 ×9	4 ×3	5 ×3	4 ×4	7 ×7	9 ×3	2 ×2	3 ×3
3.	8 ×5	6 ×4	8 ×2	9 ×7	4 ×8	7 ×3	5 ×5	9 ×8
4.	1 ×1	9 ×5	8 ×6	7 ×6	9 ×6	7 ×8	3 ×7	7 ×4
5.	6 ×3	7 ×0	4 ×9	6 ×5	2 ×7	9 ×1	3 ×9	6 ×8
6.	5 ×4	4 ×2	5 ×2	8 ×8	2 ×9	6 ×7	8 ×9	2 ×0

Lesson 4.2   Multiplying 2 Digits by 1 Digit

$$\begin{array}{r} 3\,2 \\ \times\ 3 \\ \hline 6 \end{array}$$ Multiply 2 ones by 3.
$2 \times 3 = 6$

$$\begin{array}{r} 3\,2 \\ \times\ 3 \\ \hline 9\,6 \end{array}$$ Multiply 3 tens by 3.
$30 \times 3 = 90$

Multiply.

	a	b	c	d	e	f
1.	$\begin{array}{r}23\\ \times\ 2\\ \hline\end{array}$	$\begin{array}{r}71\\ \times\ 1\\ \hline\end{array}$	$\begin{array}{r}12\\ \times\ 4\\ \hline\end{array}$	$\begin{array}{r}33\\ \times\ 2\\ \hline\end{array}$	$\begin{array}{r}10\\ \times\ 7\\ \hline\end{array}$	$\begin{array}{r}24\\ \times\ 2\\ \hline\end{array}$
2.	$\begin{array}{r}44\\ \times\ 2\\ \hline\end{array}$	$\begin{array}{r}43\\ \times\ 2\\ \hline\end{array}$	$\begin{array}{r}90\\ \times\ 1\\ \hline\end{array}$	$\begin{array}{r}22\\ \times\ 4\\ \hline\end{array}$	$\begin{array}{r}12\\ \times\ 3\\ \hline\end{array}$	$\begin{array}{r}14\\ \times\ 2\\ \hline\end{array}$
3.	$\begin{array}{r}11\\ \times\ 9\\ \hline\end{array}$	$\begin{array}{r}75\\ \times\ 1\\ \hline\end{array}$	$\begin{array}{r}11\\ \times\ 6\\ \hline\end{array}$	$\begin{array}{r}30\\ \times\ 3\\ \hline\end{array}$	$\begin{array}{r}10\\ \times\ 4\\ \hline\end{array}$	$\begin{array}{r}42\\ \times\ 2\\ \hline\end{array}$
4.	$\begin{array}{r}11\\ \times\ 7\\ \hline\end{array}$	$\begin{array}{r}10\\ \times\ 2\\ \hline\end{array}$	$\begin{array}{r}33\\ \times\ 0\\ \hline\end{array}$	$\begin{array}{r}13\\ \times\ 3\\ \hline\end{array}$	$\begin{array}{r}20\\ \times\ 3\\ \hline\end{array}$	$\begin{array}{r}31\\ \times\ 2\\ \hline\end{array}$
5.	$\begin{array}{r}10\\ \times\ 2\\ \hline\end{array}$	$\begin{array}{r}41\\ \times\ 2\\ \hline\end{array}$	$\begin{array}{r}13\\ \times\ 2\\ \hline\end{array}$	$\begin{array}{r}40\\ \times\ 2\\ \hline\end{array}$	$\begin{array}{r}30\\ \times\ 2\\ \hline\end{array}$	$\begin{array}{r}11\\ \times\ 5\\ \hline\end{array}$
6.	$\begin{array}{r}30\\ \times\ 1\\ \hline\end{array}$	$\begin{array}{r}11\\ \times\ 7\\ \hline\end{array}$	$\begin{array}{r}25\\ \times\ 1\\ \hline\end{array}$	$\begin{array}{r}42\\ \times\ 0\\ \hline\end{array}$	$\begin{array}{r}22\\ \times\ 3\\ \hline\end{array}$	$\begin{array}{r}10\\ \times\ 1\\ \hline\end{array}$
7.	$\begin{array}{r}14\\ \times\ 0\\ \hline\end{array}$	$\begin{array}{r}10\\ \times\ 5\\ \hline\end{array}$	$\begin{array}{r}31\\ \times\ 3\\ \hline\end{array}$	$\begin{array}{r}12\\ \times\ 3\\ \hline\end{array}$	$\begin{array}{r}20\\ \times\ 4\\ \hline\end{array}$	$\begin{array}{r}10\\ \times\ 7\\ \hline\end{array}$

Lesson 4.3   Multiplying 2 Digits by 1 Digit (renaming)

$$\begin{array}{r} \overset{1}{7}2 \\ \times\ 8 \\ \hline 6 \end{array}$$ Multiply 2 ones by 8.
$2 \times 8 = 16$ or $10 + 6$
6 ← Put 6 under the ones place.
Add the 10 above the 7.

$$\begin{array}{r} \overset{1}{7}2 \\ \times\ 8 \\ \hline 576 \end{array}$$ Multiply 7 tens by 8.
Then, add 1 ten.
$70 \times 8 = 560 \rightarrow 560 + 10 =$
570 or $500 + 70$

Multiply.

	a	b	c	d	e	f
1.	73 × 4	25 × 2	36 × 3	52 × 5	23 × 4	42 × 5
2.	19 × 2	26 × 2	68 × 3	54 × 5	47 × 8	33 × 4
3.	32 × 9	48 × 8	52 × 3	34 × 4	17 × 5	22 × 5
4.	66 × 3	45 × 5	66 × 5	19 × 9	38 × 9	74 × 3
5.	55 × 3	64 × 8	83 × 5	49 × 7	50 × 9	86 × 6
6.	60 × 6	17 × 3	48 × 9	75 × 3	60 × 9	96 × 5
7.	31 × 9	77 × 4	82 × 3	96 × 3	40 × 7	79 × 2

Lesson 4.4   Problem Solving

SHOW YOUR WORK

Solve each problem.

1. There are 48 chicken farms near an Ohio town. If each farm has 9 barns, how many total barns are there?

   There are _____ total barns.

2. Mr. Ferris has a canoe rental business. Over the weekend, he rented 47 canoes. A canoe holds 3 people. If each canoe was full, how many people did Mr. Ferris rent to over the weekend?

   Mr. Ferris rented to _____ people.

3. The school planned for 92 students to attend the school dance. The school bought 4 slices of pizza for each student. How many slices did the school buy?

   The school bought _____ slices.

4. The pool opened on Memorial Day. Ninety-four people showed up. The pool manager gave out 2 vouchers to each person for free drinks. How many vouchers did the pool manager give out?

   The manager gave out _____ vouchers.

5. In the Sumton community, there are 56 houses. If there are 3 children living in each house, how many children live in houses in Sumton?

   There are _____ children living in houses in Sumton.

6. Deon and Denise are saving up to buy a computer game. If they put 23 dollars a week in the bank, how much money will they have in 5 weeks?

   They will have _____ dollars.

1.	
2.	
3.	
4.	
5.	6.

Lesson 4.5 Multiplying 3 Digits by 1 Digit (renaming)

$$\begin{array}{r} \overset{1}{7}52 \\ \times\ \ 8 \\ \hline 6 \end{array}$$
Multiply 2 ones by 8.
Put 1 ten above the 5.

$$\begin{array}{r} \overset{4}{7}\overset{1}{5}2 \\ \times\ \ 8 \\ \hline 16 \end{array}$$
Multiply 5 tens by 8. Then, add 1 ten.
Put 4 hundreds above the 7.

$$\begin{array}{r} \overset{4}{7}\overset{1}{5}2 \\ \times\ \ 8 \\ \hline 6016 \end{array}$$
Multiply 7 hundreds by 8.
Then, add 4 hundreds.

Multiply.

	a	b	c	d	e	f
1.	118 × 3	305 × 4	224 × 5	152 × 3	200 × 7	137 × 5
2.	327 × 3	158 × 3	235 × 6	142 × 9	580 × 3	129 × 9
3.	335 × 5	190 × 7	421 × 8	201 × 9	287 × 3	243 × 4
4.	405 × 5	118 × 8	402 × 3	498 × 6	700 × 7	398 × 2
5.	652 × 3	142 × 4	704 × 8	193 × 7	246 × 3	152 × 7
6.	704 × 6	751 × 3	200 × 7	555 × 2	909 × 2	730 × 7

Lesson 4.6 Multiplying 2 Digits by 2 Digits

19 ×27	⁶ 19 ×27 133	Multiply 9 ones by 7. Put 6 tens above the 1. Multiply 1 ten by 7. Then, add 6 tens.	¹ 19 ×27 133 38	Multiply 9 ones by 2. Put 1 ten above the 1. Multiply 1 ten by 2. Then, add 1 ten.

$$
\begin{array}{r}
19 \\
\times 27 \\
\hline
133 \\
+38 \\
\hline
513
\end{array} \Big\} \text{Add.}
$$

Multiply.

	a	b	c	d	e	f
1.	22 ×33	11 ×45	80 ×10	31 ×23	13 ×12	30 ×31
2.	41 ×21	32 ×20	40 ×10	21 ×31	30 ×30	14 ×10
3.	22 ×44	14 ×20	40 ×12	90 ×10	13 ×13	30 ×11
4.	70 ×11	12 ×11	81 ×10	24 ×12	40 ×22	31 ×31

Lesson 4.7 Multiplying 2 Digits by 2 Digits
(with renaming)

Multiply.

	a	b	c	d	e	f
1.	22 ×19	32 ×41	72 ×18	45 ×15	48 ×20	77 ×22
2.	63 ×24	52 ×48	28 ×25	77 ×30	33 ×29	90 ×70
3.	57 ×23	18 ×18	77 ×27	65 ×17	88 ×22	90 ×20
4.	37 ×23	91 ×38	44 ×43	17 ×13	88 ×17	55 ×38

Lesson 4.8 Multiplying 3 Digits by 2 Digits (with renaming)

Multiply.

	a	b	c	d	e	f
1.	315 × 30	527 × 42	287 × 21	242 × 70	209 × 30	813 × 17
2.	140 × 32	196 × 23	673 × 92	542 × 48	604 × 40	150 × 45
3.	713 × 67	900 × 42	198 × 72	513 × 58	841 × 71	379 × 84
4.	125 × 73	706 × 31	448 × 33	809 × 12	615 × 73	458 × 83

Lesson 4.9 Multiplication Practice

Multiply.

	a	b	c	d	e	f
1.	$\begin{array}{r} 81 \\ \times\ 9 \\ \hline \end{array}$	$\begin{array}{r} 23 \\ \times\ 4 \\ \hline \end{array}$	$\begin{array}{r} 63 \\ \times\ 7 \\ \hline \end{array}$	$\begin{array}{r} 22 \\ \times\ 3 \\ \hline \end{array}$	$\begin{array}{r} 78 \\ \times\ 9 \\ \hline \end{array}$	$\begin{array}{r} 94 \\ \times\ 3 \\ \hline \end{array}$
2.	$\begin{array}{r} 90 \\ \times\ 8 \\ \hline \end{array}$	$\begin{array}{r} 36 \\ \times\ 5 \\ \hline \end{array}$	$\begin{array}{r} 52 \\ \times\ 3 \\ \hline \end{array}$	$\begin{array}{r} 44 \\ \times\ 2 \\ \hline \end{array}$	$\begin{array}{r} 73 \\ \times\ 5 \\ \hline \end{array}$	$\begin{array}{r} 87 \\ \times\ 8 \\ \hline \end{array}$
3.	$\begin{array}{r} 465 \\ \times\ 3 \\ \hline \end{array}$	$\begin{array}{r} 203 \\ \times\ 3 \\ \hline \end{array}$	$\begin{array}{r} 515 \\ \times\ 8 \\ \hline \end{array}$	$\begin{array}{r} 150 \\ \times\ 3 \\ \hline \end{array}$	$\begin{array}{r} 917 \\ \times\ 7 \\ \hline \end{array}$	$\begin{array}{r} 711 \\ \times\ 6 \\ \hline \end{array}$
4.	$\begin{array}{r} 258 \\ \times\ 4 \\ \hline \end{array}$	$\begin{array}{r} 412 \\ \times\ 3 \\ \hline \end{array}$	$\begin{array}{r} 330 \\ \times\ 3 \\ \hline \end{array}$	$\begin{array}{r} 703 \\ \times\ 6 \\ \hline \end{array}$	$\begin{array}{r} 900 \\ \times\ 9 \\ \hline \end{array}$	$\begin{array}{r} 664 \\ \times\ 8 \\ \hline \end{array}$
5.	$\begin{array}{r} 72 \\ \times 38 \\ \hline \end{array}$	$\begin{array}{r} 49 \\ \times 23 \\ \hline \end{array}$	$\begin{array}{r} 32 \\ \times 17 \\ \hline \end{array}$	$\begin{array}{r} 90 \\ \times 30 \\ \hline \end{array}$	$\begin{array}{r} 84 \\ \times\ 7 \\ \hline \end{array}$	$\begin{array}{r} 68 \\ \times 32 \\ \hline \end{array}$
6.	$\begin{array}{r} 27 \\ \times 18 \\ \hline \end{array}$	$\begin{array}{r} 80 \\ \times 22 \\ \hline \end{array}$	$\begin{array}{r} 77 \\ \times 43 \\ \hline \end{array}$	$\begin{array}{r} 52 \\ \times 30 \\ \hline \end{array}$	$\begin{array}{r} 19 \\ \times 17 \\ \hline \end{array}$	$\begin{array}{r} 48 \\ \times 27 \\ \hline \end{array}$

Lesson 4.10 Problem Solving

Solve each problem.

1. Xavier loves to eat pears. He ate 2 a day for 48 days. How many pears did Xavier eat?

   Xavier ate _____ pears.

2. Clayton keeps pet mice. If his 33 mice have 12 babies each, how many mice will Clayton have in all?

   Clayton will have _____ mice.

3. In a tropical rain forest, the average annual rainfall is about 150 inches. After 5 years, about how much rain will have fallen in the rain forest?

   About _____ inches of rain will have fallen.

4. A class of 55 students went on a field trip to collect seashells. If the students collected 15 shells each, how many shells did they collect?

   The students collected _____ shells.

5. Buses were reserved for the big field trip. If each bus holds 20 students, how many students would 6 buses hold?

   The buses would hold _____ students.

6. If 16 potato chips is a serving size and there are 5 servings per bag, how many potato chips are in each bag?

   There are _____ chips in a bag.

1.

2.

3.

4.

5.

6.

Check What You Learned

Multiplying through 3 Digits by 2 Digits

Multiply.

	a	b	c	d	e	f	g
1.	72 × 4	24 × 8	339 × 2	34 × 8	150 × 9	333 × 2	93 × 2
2.	242 × 2	64 × 8	31 × 7	300 × 21	7 ×9	173 × 28	90 × 8
3.	8 ×7	728 × 1	22 × 3	207 × 21	900 × 6	79 × 4	643 × 7
4.	743 × 2	439 × 10	117 × 23	943 × 6	8 ×6	200 × 9	555 × 40
5.	42 ×41	311 × 12	72 ×18	12 ×11	507 × 42	95 ×27	353 × 17
6.	606 × 12	786 × 31	202 × 33	52 ×49	86 ×14	94 ×65	403 × 55

NAME _____

Check What You Learned

Multiplying through 3 Digits by 2 Digits

Solve each problem.

7. Mrs. Rockwell checked on how much time her students spend doing homework. If all 23 students spend 20 hours a week, how much homework do the students do in a week?

They do _____ hours of homework a week.

8. A cable program loans channel boxes to 21 community centers for a trial program. If there are 12 boxes for each center, how many boxes are being loaned?

There are _____ boxes being loaned.

9. A girls' club is trying to get into the record books for the most hair braids. There are 372 girls. If each girl braids her hair into 40 little braids, how many braids will they have?

They will have _____ braids.

10. In one week, Pop sold ice cream cones to 375 people. If each customer had 2 scoops, how many scoops did Pop sell?

Pop sold _____ scoops of ice cream.

11. Mrs. Numkena's science class raised tadpoles. If 35 students raised 23 tadpoles each, how many tadpoles did the class have?

The class had _____ tadpoles.

12. At Lakeside View, 15 apartment houses were built. If there are 12 units to each apartment house, how many units are available?

There are _____ units available.

7.

8.

9.

10.

11.

12.

CHAPTER 4 POSTTEST

Check What You Know

Division Facts through 81 ÷ 9

Divide.

	a	b	c	d	e
1.	3)15	7)49	9)27	5)45	7)21
2.	3)18	7)42	9)81	7)56	6)30
3.	4)36	4)16	5)40	2)10	4)36
4.	9)18	5)35	7)28	2)6	4)24
5.	5)15	3)21	9)54	2)8	2)14
6.	6)36	6)48	8)32	3)24	3)9
7.	8)72	8)64	5)25	9)9	3)0
8.	5)35	5)20	4)36	8)56	2)12
9.	2)18	3)27	4)28	2)2	2)8
10.	3)15	9)63	6)48	7)14	9)27

Check What You Know

SHOW YOUR WORK

Division Facts through 81 ÷ 9

Solve each problem.

11. Lori found 42 shells at the beach. She gave the same number of shells to 7 of her friends. How many shells did she give to each friend?

She gave _____ shells to each friend.

12. The drama club is giving a party in the school lunchroom. The club wants to be seated in groups of 8. If 64 students go to the party, how many groups of students will there be?

The drama club will have _____ groups of students.

13. The Pancake Restaurant served 32 pancakes. If 8 customers ate an equal number of pancakes, how many did each person eat?

Each person ate _____ pancakes each.

14. In the flower seed package, there are 48 seeds. Alicia has 8 flowerpots. She wants to put an equal number of seeds in each pot. How many seeds should she put in each pot?

She should put _____ seeds in each pot.

15. The local team has a supply of 54 baseballs for 9 home games. How many baseballs are available for each home game?

There are _____ baseballs available for each home game.

16. The class gerbil has just had 16 babies. If there are 8 students who want to take them home, how many babies can each student have?

Each student can have _____ baby gerbils.

11.	
12.	
13.	**14.**
15.	**16.**

Lesson 5.1   Dividing through 45 ÷ 5

9 ←———— quotient

divisor ———→ $5\overline{)45}$ ←———— dividend

5-column ———→ ↓ (divisors)

To check your answer, do the inverse operation.

If $45 ÷ 5 = 9$, then $5 × 9 = 45$ must be true.

Using the division table, find 45 in the 5 column. The quotient is named at the beginning of the row.

(quotients)

quotient ———→

x	0	1	2	3	4	5	6	7	8	9
0	0	0	0	0	0	0	0	0	0	0
1	0	1	2	3	4	5	6	7	8	9
2	0	2	4	6	8	10	12	14	16	18
3	0	3	6	9	12	15	18	21	24	27
4	0	4	8	12	16	20	24	28	32	36
5	0	5	10	15	20	25	30	35	40	45
6	0	6	12	18	24	30	36	42	48	54
7	0	7	14	21	28	35	42	49	56	63
8	0	8	16	24	32	40	48	56	64	72
9	0	9	18	27	36	45	54	63	72	81

Divide.

	a	b	c	d	e	f
1.	$5\overline{)35}$	$4\overline{)16}$	$4\overline{)36}$	$3\overline{)18}$	$5\overline{)25}$	$4\overline{)28}$
2.	$2\overline{)18}$	$3\overline{)18}$	$3\overline{)27}$	$3\overline{)12}$	$5\overline{)20}$	$3\overline{)21}$
3.	$5\overline{)45}$	$3\overline{)15}$	$5\overline{)30}$	$4\overline{)32}$	$2\overline{)8}$	$2\overline{)10}$
4.	$2\overline{)16}$	$2\overline{)12}$	$9\overline{)45}$	$5\overline{)35}$	$2\overline{)18}$	$5\overline{)40}$
5.	$5\overline{)30}$	$4\overline{)24}$	$3\overline{)24}$	$4\overline{)20}$	$3\overline{)9}$	$4\overline{)12}$
6.	$2\overline{)14}$	$4\overline{)4}$	$5\overline{)15}$	$5\overline{)10}$	$4\overline{)0}$	$3\overline{)6}$

Complete the following.

	a	b	c	d
7.	$\begin{array}{r} 5 \\ \times\ 3 \\ \hline 15 \end{array}$ so $3\overline{)15}$	$\begin{array}{r} 4 \\ \times\ 7 \\ \hline 28 \end{array}$ so $7\overline{)28}$	$\begin{array}{r} 3 \\ \times\ 4 \\ \hline 12 \end{array}$ so $4\overline{)12}$	$\begin{array}{r} 9 \\ \times\ 2 \\ \hline 18 \end{array}$ so $2\overline{)18}$

Lesson 5.2 Dividing through 63 ÷ 7

$$\text{divisor} \longrightarrow 7\overline{)63} \begin{array}{l} \longleftarrow \text{quotient} \\ \longleftarrow \text{dividend} \end{array}$$

To check your answer, do the inverse operation.

If 63 ÷ 7 = 9, then 7 × 9 = 63 must be true.

Using the division table, find 63 in the 7 column. The quotient is named at the end of the row.

7-column

x	0	1	2	3	4	5	6	7	8	9
0	0	0	0	0	0	0	0	0	0	0
1	0	1	2	3	4	5	6	7	8	9
2	0	2	4	6	8	10	12	14	16	18
3	0	3	6	9	12	15	18	21	24	27
4	0	4	8	12	16	20	24	28	32	36
5	0	5	10	15	20	25	30	35	40	45
6	0	6	12	18	24	30	36	42	48	54
7	0	7	14	21	28	35	42	49	56	63
8	0	8	16	24	32	40	48	56	64	72
9	0	9	18	27	36	45	54	63	72	81

quotient

Divide.

	a	b	c	d	e	f
1.	7)49	5)45	6)36	3)24	3)27	4)28
2.	2)18	4)24	6)48	4)32	5)45	2)16
3.	5)40	2)12	6)6	7)56	7)0	6)54
4.	5)25	5)10	7)21	7)28	6)42	7)63
5.	6)24	4)20	7)35	5)30	4)12	4)16
6.	7)7	5)15	7)42	3)21	6)12	6)30

Complete the following.

	a	b	c
7.	$\begin{array}{r} 7 \\ \times\ 6 \\ \hline 42 \end{array}$ so 6)42	$\begin{array}{r} 4 \\ \times\ 6 \\ \hline 24 \end{array}$ so 6)24	$\begin{array}{r} 8 \\ \times\ 7 \\ \hline 56 \end{array}$ so 7)56

Lesson 5.3 Dividing through 81 ÷ 9

$$\begin{array}{r} 9 \longleftarrow \text{quotient} \\ \text{divisor} \longrightarrow 9\overline{)81} \longleftarrow \text{dividend} \end{array}$$

To check your answer, do the inverse operation.

If $81 \div 9 = 9$, then $9 \times 9 = 81$ must be true.

Using the division table, find 81 in the 9 column. The quotient is named at the end of the row.

9-column

x	0	1	2	3	4	5	6	7	8	9
0	0	0	0	0	0	0	0	0	0	0
1	0	1	2	3	4	5	6	7	8	9
2	0	2	4	6	8	10	12	14	16	18
3	0	3	6	9	12	15	18	21	24	27
4	0	4	8	12	16	20	24	28	32	36
5	0	5	10	15	20	25	30	35	40	45
6	0	6	12	18	24	30	36	42	48	54
7	0	7	14	21	28	35	42	49	56	63
8	0	8	16	24	32	40	48	56	64	72
9	0	9	18	27	36	45	54	63	72	81

quotient

Divide.

	a	b	c	d	e	f
1.	$9\overline{)72}$	$8\overline{)40}$	$8\overline{)24}$	$6\overline{)48}$	$7\overline{)28}$	$6\overline{)36}$
2.	$6\overline{)18}$	$3\overline{)21}$	$7\overline{)49}$	$9\overline{)54}$	$9\overline{)81}$	$4\overline{)32}$
3.	$5\overline{)35}$	$7\overline{)56}$	$9\overline{)18}$	$7\overline{)42}$	$9\overline{)36}$	$7\overline{)28}$
4.	$9\overline{)45}$	$5\overline{)30}$	$4\overline{)12}$	$5\overline{)25}$	$7\overline{)14}$	$9\overline{)0}$
5.	$9\overline{)9}$	$8\overline{)40}$	$8\overline{)48}$	$6\overline{)42}$	$3\overline{)27}$	$4\overline{)28}$

Complete the following.

	a	b	c

6.
$$\begin{array}{r} 7 \\ \times\ 5 \\ \hline 35 \end{array} \text{ so } 5\overline{)35} \qquad \begin{array}{r} 8 \\ \times\ 8 \\ \hline 64 \end{array} \text{ so } 8\overline{)64} \qquad \begin{array}{r} 9 \\ \times\ 6 \\ \hline 54 \end{array} \text{ so } 6\overline{)54}$$

7.
$$\begin{array}{r} 9 \\ \times\ 4 \\ \hline 36 \end{array} \text{ so } 4\overline{)36} \qquad \begin{array}{r} 6 \\ \times\ 4 \\ \hline 24 \end{array} \text{ so } 4\overline{)24} \qquad \begin{array}{r} 6 \\ \times\ 8 \\ \hline 48 \end{array} \text{ so } 8\overline{)48}$$

Lesson 5.4 Division Practice

Divide.

	a	b	c	d	e
1.	8)56	6)24	2)18	5)35	7)42
2.	6)48	6)30	8)72	6)36	9)81
3.	9)54	3)21	7)28	3)18	2)18
4.	5)45	9)36	6)42	8)64	7)63
5.	3)24	9)27	5)20	7)49	5)25
6.	5)40	7)14	9)81	9)0	4)16

Lesson 5.5   Problem Solving

SHOW YOUR WORK

Solve each problem.

1. Eddie and Toru listened to 72 of their favorite songs. If there were 9 songs on each CD, how many CDs did they listen to?

   They listened to _____ CDs.

2. Mr. Luiz printed 35 tests for his students. If there were 7 rows of students, how many tests were passed out to each row?

   There were _____ tests passed out to each row.

3. Gary opened a bag of candy containing 81 pieces. He wants to give each of his guests the same number of pieces. If he has 9 guests, how many pieces does each person get?

   Each guest gets _____ pieces.

4. Last year, Mrs. Ford decided to give chores to each person in the family. Each person got the same number of chores. There are 8 family members. If there were 32 chores, how many did each person get?

   Each person got _____ chores.

5. It takes 16 hours to drive to the dunes. Tasha and her brother Kurt will drive the same number of hours. How many hours will each of them drive?

   Each of them will drive _____ hours.

6. The Pet Warehouse received 63 boxes of cat litter. The same number of boxes will be sent to 9 stores. How many boxes will each store get?

   Each store will get _____ boxes.

1.

2.

3.

4.

5.   6.

Lesson 5.6 Problem Solving

Solve each problem.

1. Mrs. Blair is planning a yard party. Her big punch bowl holds 40 glasses of punch. If she wants to allow 5 glasses for each guest, how many guests will the punch bowl serve?

   The punch bowl will serve _____ guests.

2. At the rodeo, 32 people signed up for bronco riding. The 4 horses will give the same number of rides. How many rides will each horse give?

   Each horse will give _____ rides.

3. Mr. Ferris is packing to move to a new house. He has 35 pairs of shoes. He can pack 7 pairs of shoes in a box. How many boxes will he need for his shoes?

   Mr. Ferris will need _____ boxes for his shoes.

4. At the local fair, 72 people waited in line for a boat ride. The boat can hold 8 people. How many trips will the boat have to take for everyone to get a ride?

   The boat will have to take _____ trips.

5. The Davis brothers found 27 cars when they cleaned out their toy closet. They want to give the same number of cars to each of their 3 cousins. How many cars will each cousin get?

   Each cousin will get _____ toy cars.

6. Mrs. Gomez sold 18 pet lizards this week at her pet store. If 9 customers bought the same number of lizards, how many lizards did each person take home?

   Each person took home _____ lizards.

1.	
2.	
3.	
4.	
5.	6.

Check What You Learned

Division Facts through 81 ÷ 9

Divide.

	a	b	c	d	e
1.	3)18	9)27	7)7	8)64	5)40
2.	9)72	6)36	8)16	7)21	4)28
3.	5)25	8)64	9)54	5)35	3)12
4.	7)49	9)9	7)21	2)18	3)18
5.	4)16	4)20	9)36	8)56	7)42
6.	9)0	4)32	9)81	5)10	7)49
7.	8)32	9)54	6)48	3)24	4)24
8.	9)45	3)27	5)30	6)42	2)4
9.	8)40	9)63	2)14	3)9	7)56
10.	8)48	7)7	2)8	1)9	7)28

Check What You Learned

SHOW YOUR WORK

Division Facts through 81 ÷ 9

Solve each problem.

11. A group of 7 boys cut lawns over the weekend. They made 56 dollars. Each boy will make the same amount. How much money will each boy get?

Each boy will get _____ dollars.

12. Gloria decided to make lemonade for her family. There are 8 people in her family. The pitcher will hold 24 glasses of lemonade. How many glasses can each person have?

Each person can have _____ glasses.

13. Susan, Marta, and Aisha have 5 hours to spend at the zoo. There are 40 different animals they want to see. During each hour at the zoo, how many animals should they plan to see?

They should plan to see _____ different animals each hour.

14. Awan and his three friends love to eat cookies. After school one day, the 4 of them ate 36 cookies. Each boy took the same number of cookies from the bag. How many cookies did each boy eat?

Each boy ate _____ cookies.

15. Venus has 21 crayons. Each crayon is a different color. If she places 3 colors in each group, how many groups of colors would she have?

She had _____ groups of colors.

16. Mr. and Mrs. Greenheart run a store. They work 63 hours every week. If they work 7 days each week, how many hours do they work every day?

They work _____ hours every day.

11.

12.

13.

14.

15.   **16.**

Check What You Know

Dividing 2 and 3 Digits by 1 Digit

Divide.

	a	b	c	d	e
1.	2)42	2)15	2)142	3)63	3)180
2.	5)152	3)521	8)55	7)70	4)98
3.	9)87	7)77	2)50	2)175	3)900
4.	3)45	5)105	5)650	8)78	3)68
5.	5)905	6)121	7)62	7)22	2)90

Check What You Know

SHOW YOUR WORK

Dividing 2 and 3 Digits by 1 Digit

Solve each problem.

6. The school office received 22 computers. If there are 9 classrooms receiving the computers, how many computers will go to each classroom? How many computers will be left?

Each classroom will receive _____ computers.

There will be _____ extra computers.

7. There are 234 summer jobs for lifeguards at the city pools. There will be 3 lifeguards at each city pool. How many city pools are there?

There are _____ city pools.

8. At the Hot Dog Shack, customers bought 27 hot dogs on Saturday. There were only 9 customers. How many hot dogs did each customer buy?

Each customer bought _____ hot dogs.

9. The school spirit club baked cakes for a charity event. There were 75 different types of cakes. Each baker baked the same number of cakes. If there were 5 bakers, how many cakes did each baker make?

Each baker made _____ cakes.

10. The Fish Shop is open 72 hours a week. The shop is open 6 days a week and the same number of hours each day. How many hours each day is the shop open?

The shop is open _____ hours a day.

11. The glee club needs to sell 382 tickets to win a trip. If there are 8 members who want to go on the trip, how many tickets does each member need to sell? How many extra tickets are left?

Each member needs to sell _____ tickets.

There will be _____ extra tickets.

6.

7.

8.

9.

10.   **11.**

Lesson 6.1 Dividing 2 Digits

x	1	2	3	4	5
8	8	16	24	32	40

$$8\overline{)33}$$ gives 4

$8 \times 4 \quad -32$
Subtract. $\quad 1$

33 is between 32 and 40, so 33 ÷ 8 is between 4 and 5. The ones digit is 4.

Since 33 − 32 = 1 and 1 is less than 8, the remainder 1 is recorded like this: ⟶

$$8\overline{)33} \quad 4\ r\ 1$$
$$-32$$
$$1$$

Divide.

	a	b	c	d	e
1.	5)26	7)58	4)31	9)82	6)35
2.	8)66	3)17	2)13	7)50	6)40
3.	9)30	5)41	3)10	8)73	7)57
4.	8)20	6)37	9)55	7)29	5)47

Lesson 6.1 Dividing 2 Digits

$$\begin{array}{c|c|c|c} x & 10 & 20 & 30 \\ \hline 3 & 30 & 60 & 90 \end{array}$$

$$3 \times 20 \quad \begin{array}{r} 2 \\ 3\overline{)67} \\ -60 \\ \hline \end{array}$$
Subtract.   7

67 is between 60 and 90, so 67 ÷ 3 is between 20 and 30. The tens digit is 2.

$$\begin{array}{c|c|c|c} x & 1 & 2 & 3 \\ \hline 3 & 3 & 6 & 9 \end{array}$$

$$\begin{array}{r} 22 \text{ r } 1 \\ 3\overline{)67} \\ -60 \\ \hline 7 \\ -6 \\ \hline 1 \end{array}$$

3 × 2 = 6, so the ones is 2.

7 − 6 = 1, so the remainder is 1.

3 × 2

Subtract.

Divide.

	a	b	c	d	e
1.	2)36	5)76	7)79	4)96	7)93
2.	5)86	3)96	8)99	7)84	3)75
3.	6)93	6)72	8)89	7)89	9)99
4.	4)88	3)84	2)77	4)78	8)93

Lesson 6.2 Division Practice

Divide.

	a	b	c	d	e
1.	2)63	5)75	9)97	7)88	5)56
2.	3)72	8)96	6)78	4)65	5)97
3.	2)75	4)34	6)93	8)89	2)69
4.	3)64	7)87	5)95	4)47	3)59
5.	4)59	6)71	2)49	7)99	8)97

Lesson 6.2 Problem Solving

Solve each problem.

6. Ms. Garrett had 40 guests at her birthday party. She cut her cake into 88 slices. Each guest ate 2 pieces of cake. How many slices were left?

   There were _____ slices left.

7. Lucy babysits for 2 families. She works the same number of hours each month for each family. If she worked 76 hours last month, how many hours did she work for each family?

   She worked _____ hours for each family.

8. Tom and Jose enjoy playing video games. Together they play 10 hours a week. If they play 5 days a week, how many hours a day do they both play together?

   They play together _____ hours a day.

9. At the basketball tournament, 28 people signed up to play. If there were 4 teams, how many players were on a team?

   There were _____ players on each team.

10. The hardware store received 95 nails. The nails go in four drawers. Each drawer will hold the same number of nails. How many nails will fit in each drawer? How many nails will be left over?

    _____ nails will fit in each drawer.

    There will be _____ extra nails.

| 6. |
| 7. |
| 8. |

| 9. | 10. |

NAME _____

Lesson 6.3 Dividing 3 Digits

Since $100 \times 8 = 800$ and 800 is greater than 453, there is no hundred digit.

$$8\overline{)453}$$

x	10	20	30	40	50	60
8	80	160	240	320	400	480

453 is between 400 and 480. $453 \div 8$ is between 50 and 60. The tens digit is 5.

$$\begin{array}{r} 5 \\ 8\overline{)453} \\ -40 \quad 8 \times 5 = 40 \\ \hline 53 \text{ Subtract} \end{array}$$

x	1	2	3	4	5	6	7
8	8	16	24	32	40	48	56

53 is between 48 and 56. $53 \div 8$ is between 6 and 7. The ones digit is 6.

$$\begin{array}{r} 56 \text{ r } 5 \\ 8\overline{)453} \\ -40 \\ \hline 53 \quad 8 \times 6 = 48 \\ -48 \quad \text{Subtract} \\ \hline 5 \quad \text{Remainder} \end{array}$$

Divide.

	a	b	c	d	e
1.	$8\overline{)720}$	$4\overline{)372}$	$9\overline{)372}$	$4\overline{)173}$	$2\overline{)150}$
2.	$6\overline{)552}$	$3\overline{)139}$	$4\overline{)248}$	$9\overline{)890}$	$5\overline{)105}$
3.	$9\overline{)780}$	$5\overline{)225}$	$9\overline{)813}$	$7\overline{)511}$	$3\overline{)110}$

Lesson 6.3 Dividing 3 Digits

x	100	200
6	600	1200

713 is between 600 and 1200, so 713 ÷ 6 is between 100 and 200. The hundreds digit is 1.

```
      1
  6) 7 1 3
   - 6 0 0    100 × 6
  ─────────
     1 1 3    Subtract
```

x	10	20
6	60	120

113 is between 60 and 120, so 113 ÷ 6 is between 10 and 20. The tens digit is 1.

```
     1 1
  6) 7 1 3
   - 6 0 0
  ─────────
     1 1 3
    -  6 0    10 × 6
  ─────────
       5 3    Subtract
```

x	1	2	3	4	5	6	7	8	9
6	6	12	18	24	30	36	42	48	54

53 is between 48 and 54, so 53 ÷ 6 is between 8 and 9. The ones digit is 8.

```
     1 1 8 r 5
  6) 7 1 3
   - 6 0 0
  ─────────
     1 1 3
    -  6 0
  ─────────
       5 3    8 × 6 = 48
    -  4 8    Subtract
  ─────────
         5    Remainder
```

Divide.

	a	b	c	d	e
1.	5)546	4)762	3)472	6)687	8)994
2.	3)933	4)456	7)806	2)451	5)750
3.	9)936	3)768	9)915	4)848	6)762
4.	2)835	2)352	7)766	4)506	2)284

Lesson 6.4 Division Practice

Divide.

	a	b	c	d	e
1.	6)773	2)898	4)566	6)781	3)972
2.	2)317	4)732	9)989	7)897	2)394
3.	5)529	8)897	3)676	2)348	6)930
4.	3)784	5)788	3)481	5)558	2)610
5.	3)324	5)953	4)868	3)975	6)720

Lesson 6.4 Problem Solving

Solve each problem.

6. The cross-country team runs about 110 miles a week. If they stop for a break about every 7 miles, how many breaks do they take each week?

They take _____ breaks each week.

6.

7. The pool's lap lane is 675 feet long. If a swimmer splits this length into 4 equal sections, how many feet will each section be? How many feet are left to swim?

There are _____ feet in each section.

There are _____ feet left to swim.

7.

8. The garden show is moving into a bigger area. The new space has 935 square feet of space for displays. There are 16 different displays, and each display will need the same amount of space. How many square feet does each display get? How many square feet are left over?

Each display gets _____ square feet of space.

There are _____ square feet of space left over.

8.

9. A boys' club picked up litter in the park. They collected 913 bags of litter. If each boy collected about the same amount, about how many bags did the 7 boys collect? How many extra bags were collected?

Each boy picked up about _____ bags.

There were _____ extra bags collected.

9. | **10.**

10. The school supply store received a shipment of 730 pens. If the pens are packed in 5 boxes, how many pens are in each box?

There are _____ pens in each box.

Check What You Learned

Dividing 2 and 3 Digits by 1 Digit

Divide.

	a	b	c	d	e
1.	2)32	3)321	3)49	8)97	2)178
2.	4)121	6)798	5)557	6)636	8)889
3.	2)96	3)87	8)93	3)42	7)31
4.	8)75	2)19	8)43	9)89	3)66
5.	3)603	5)917	6)762	7)37	2)48

Check What You Learned

Dividing 2 and 3 Digits by 1 Digit

Solve each problem.

6. Howard Jackson scored 158 points this season playing basketball. He played in 7 games and scored about the same number of points in each game. About how many points did he score in each game? How many points are left over?

He scored about _____ points in each game.

There are _____ points left over.

7. Miss Gomez drove 256 miles in 4 hours. She drove the same number of miles each hour. How many miles did she drive in 1 hour?

She drove _____ miles in 1 hour.

8. In the past 6 weeks, Jackson worked on 738 computers. Each week, he worked on the same number of computers. How many computers did he work on every week?

He worked on _____ computers every week.

9. At baseball practice, 325 pitches were thrown to the players. If 5 players got the same number of pitches, how many pitches did each player get?

Each player got _____ pitches.

10. Taylor needs 612 more dollars to buy a plane ticket to visit his cousin in Australia. If he saves 9 dollars a day, how soon can he go to Australia?

He will have the rest of the money in _____ days.

11. The bait shop ordered 136 fishing worms for their customers. The workers put them into 8 separate cups. How many worms are in each cup?

There are _____ worms in each cup.

6.	7.
8.	**9.**
10.	**11.**

Mid-Test Chapters 1–6

Add or subtract.

	a	b	c	d	e
1.	23 + 2	33 + 6	17 + 2	32 + 7	61 + 5
2.	14 + 5	73 + 1	80 + 9	52 + 7	71 + 8
3.	23 + 7	82 + 9	74 + 7	31 + 9	33 + 8
4.	38 + 5	57 + 8	86 + 8	72 + 9	24 + 9
5.	32 - 1	86 -14	25 -15	87 -34	97 -65
6.	74 - 8	93 - 9	17 - 8	63 - 8	38 -19
7.	52 +17	32 17 +10	37 +25	43 21 +18	73 +26
8.	36 +13	75 +18	41 +39	57 +18	37 +28
9.	320 - 18	715 - 23	287 - 78	555 - 98	408 - 19
10.	973 - 84	578 - 99	300 - 17	542 - 80	663 - 74

Mid-Test Chapters 1–6

Write each number in expanded form.

	a	**b**	**c**
11.	732	32,132	4,790
12.	1,003	2,314,732	3,001

Round each number to the place named.

	a	**b**	**c**
13.	13,573 hundreds	75,319 ten thousands	1,932,710 millions
14.	4,935 tens	357,013 hundred thousands	4,015 tens

Compare each pair of numbers. Write either >, <, or =.

	a	**b**	**c**
15.	13,702 ___ 13,207	3,976 ___ 9,362	932 ___ nine hundred-one
16.	26,314 ___ 260,314	978 ___ 978	3,721,460 ___ 3,710,460

Add.

	a	**b**	**c**	**d**	**e**
17.	703 +172	665 +118	713 +375	511 +430	300 +479
18.	2314 + 718	1725 + 625	3201 +1405	7358 +1757	8101 +1709

Mid-Test Chapters 1–6

Subtract.

	a	b	c	d	e
19.	32146 − 3132	67315 −14305	40195 − 9186	75532 −21530	25789 − 6642
20.	17315 − 8904	98789 −73979	42804 −38709	87897 −58898	34932 −17983

Add.

21.	4132 714 + 304	32015 + 7932	8215 1730 +1045	25713 +13846	3014 1246 + 710
22.	83548 + 8162	2315 1215 720 + 214	37805 +12125	7300 715 243 + 120	71042 + 8925

Estimate each sum or difference.

23.	5614 +3293	26417 + 2815	4932 + 512	108765 + 2046	45059 +38712
24.	32564 − 2198	4397 −2810	39702 − 615	32084 −18093	9327 − 452

CHAPTERS 1–6 MID-TEST

Mid-Test Chapters 1–6

Multiply.

	a	b	c	d	e
25.	$\begin{array}{r} 7 \\ \times 8 \\ \hline \end{array}$	$\begin{array}{r} 9 \\ \times 4 \\ \hline \end{array}$	$\begin{array}{r} 7 \\ \times 4 \\ \hline \end{array}$	$\begin{array}{r} 8 \\ \times 6 \\ \hline \end{array}$	$\begin{array}{r} 21 \\ \times\ 4 \\ \hline \end{array}$
26.	$\begin{array}{r} 32 \\ \times\ 3 \\ \hline \end{array}$	$\begin{array}{r} 14 \\ \times\ 2 \\ \hline \end{array}$	$\begin{array}{r} 44 \\ \times\ 2 \\ \hline \end{array}$	$\begin{array}{r} 12 \\ \times\ 4 \\ \hline \end{array}$	$\begin{array}{r} 20 \\ \times\ 4 \\ \hline \end{array}$
27.	$\begin{array}{r} 32 \\ \times\ 7 \\ \hline \end{array}$	$\begin{array}{r} 47 \\ \times\ 3 \\ \hline \end{array}$	$\begin{array}{r} 21 \\ \times\ 8 \\ \hline \end{array}$	$\begin{array}{r} 40 \\ \times\ 9 \\ \hline \end{array}$	$\begin{array}{r} 17 \\ \times\ 9 \\ \hline \end{array}$
28.	$\begin{array}{r} 48 \\ \times\ 7 \\ \hline \end{array}$	$\begin{array}{r} 72 \\ \times\ 8 \\ \hline \end{array}$	$\begin{array}{r} 84 \\ \times\ 4 \\ \hline \end{array}$	$\begin{array}{r} 25 \\ \times\ 7 \\ \hline \end{array}$	$\begin{array}{r} 49 \\ \times\ 9 \\ \hline \end{array}$

	a	b	c	d	e	f
29.	$\begin{array}{r} 11 \\ \times 10 \\ \hline \end{array}$	$\begin{array}{r} 22 \\ \times 11 \\ \hline \end{array}$	$\begin{array}{r} 31 \\ \times 32 \\ \hline \end{array}$	$\begin{array}{r} 43 \\ \times 20 \\ \hline \end{array}$	$\begin{array}{r} 50 \\ \times 10 \\ \hline \end{array}$	$\begin{array}{r} 31 \\ \times 20 \\ \hline \end{array}$
30.	$\begin{array}{r} 75 \\ \times 25 \\ \hline \end{array}$	$\begin{array}{r} 32 \\ \times 18 \\ \hline \end{array}$	$\begin{array}{r} 132 \\ \times\ 41 \\ \hline \end{array}$	$\begin{array}{r} 81 \\ \times 37 \\ \hline \end{array}$	$\begin{array}{r} 103 \\ \times\ 17 \\ \hline \end{array}$	$\begin{array}{r} 282 \\ \times\ 38 \\ \hline \end{array}$
31.	$\begin{array}{r} 418 \\ \times\ 45 \\ \hline \end{array}$	$\begin{array}{r} 500 \\ \times\ 32 \\ \hline \end{array}$	$\begin{array}{r} 199 \\ \times\ 47 \\ \hline \end{array}$	$\begin{array}{r} 578 \\ \times\ 23 \\ \hline \end{array}$	$\begin{array}{r} 887 \\ \times\ 52 \\ \hline \end{array}$	$\begin{array}{r} 399 \\ \times\ 19 \\ \hline \end{array}$

Mid-Test   Chapters 1–6

Divide.

	a	b	c	d	e
32.	9)81	7)56	8)48	8)64	7)42
33.	8)24	5)35	7)28	6)54	9)72
34.	3)330	2)642	7)721	4)484	8)864
35.	8)724	7)639	5)525	6)247	2)876
36.	9)458	7)807	6)684	3)949	4)713
37.	9)908	2)510	4)648	8)888	6)445

Mid-Test Chapters 1–6

Solve each problem.

38. A total of 68 hikers went on a trip to Blue Hill Mountain. If 32 of the hikers were boys, how many hikers were girls?

_____ hikers were girls.

39. On a trip to Washington, D.C., there were 33 fifth-graders and 27 fourth-graders. How many students were on the trip?

There were _____ students on the trip.

40. At the picnic grove, bird watchers saw 42 robins looking for worms. If there were 5 times as many starlings as robins, how many starlings were there?

There were _____ starlings.

41. A group of friends is getting ready for a hike at night. Each of their flashlights take 4 batteries. If they have 72 batteries, how many flashlights can they take?

They can take _____ flashlights.

Estimate your answer.

42. There are 21 members of the soccer team on the bus. If each player carries on 4 pieces of equipment, about how many pieces of equipment are on the bus?

There are about _____ pieces of equipment on the bus.

43. At the high school, all textbooks must be turned in at the end of the year. There are 150 science books, 125 math books, and 107 Spanish books. About how many books will be turned in?

About _____ books will be turned in.

38.	39.

40.

41.

42.

43.

Check What You Know

Fractions, Decimals, and Money

What fraction of each figure is shaded?

| a | b | c |

1. _____   _____   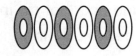 _____

What fraction of each set is shaded?

2.  _____   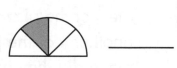 _____   888 _____

Compare each set of fractions. Use >, <, or =.

| a | b | c | d |

3. $\frac{3}{4}$ ___ $\frac{1}{4}$ $\frac{1}{2}$ ___ $\frac{2}{4}$ $\frac{7}{8}$ ___ $\frac{2}{8}$ $\frac{2}{8}$ ___ $\frac{4}{8}$

Add the fractions.

4. $\frac{1}{2} + \frac{1}{2} =$ ___ $\frac{3}{8} + \frac{2}{8} =$ ___ $\frac{1}{4} + \frac{1}{4} =$ ___ $\frac{2}{6} + \frac{1}{6} =$ ___

Subtract the fractions.

5. $\frac{7}{8} - \frac{2}{8} =$ ___ $\frac{3}{4} - \frac{2}{4} =$ ___ $\frac{2}{7} - \frac{2}{7} =$ ___ $\frac{4}{4} - \frac{2}{4} =$ ___

Add or subtract.

| a | b | c | d | e |

6.
```
   0.3 1        0.7 5       0.0 0 3      $ 7.5 0      $ 1.0 5
 + 0.2 0      + 0.1 1      + 0.7 2 0    +    .2 5    +   1.0 3
```

7.
```
   0.5 2        0.8 3       $ 1 5.2 3    $ 1 2 5.1 3     0.5 0 3
 - 0.0 8      - 0.5 2      -      7.1 7  -     5 0.0 0  - 0.4 1 0
```

NAME _____

Check What You Know

Fractions, Decimals, and Money

Solve each problem.

8. Alberta and Alicia had pizza at a sleepover. They ate $\frac{1}{4}$ of the pizza before going to sleep. They ate another $\frac{1}{4}$ of the pizza in the morning. How much pizza did they eat?

They ate _____ of the pizza.

9. It rained $\frac{1}{8}$ of an inch in June and $\frac{3}{8}$ of an inch in July. How much more rain fell in July than in June?

It rained _____ inch more in July.

10. Yesterday, Mrs. Hughes gave $\frac{3}{8}$ of her mid-term test. If she gives $\frac{2}{8}$ of the test today, how much of the test will she have given?

She will have given _____ of the test.

11. Ilia sold her skates for $34.50. She bought them a year ago for $35. How much money did Ilia lose selling her skates?

Ilia lost _____.

12. The Rollins triplets pooled their money to get their father a birthday gift. Ron had $7.36, Kyle had $15.20, and Sarah had $9.40. How much money did they have to spend on the gift?

They had_____ to spend.

13. Akira wanted to add up his change. In his left pocket, he found 32 cents. In his right pocket, he found 75 cents. How much money did he have in all?

He had _____ in change.

8.

9.

10.

11.

12.

13.

Lesson 7.1 Parts of a Whole

This diamond has four equal parts.

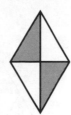

The shaded parts of this figure are shown below as the numerator of a fraction. Because 2 parts are shaded, 2 is the numerator.

$$\frac{2}{4} \longleftarrow \text{numerator}$$

$$\overline{4} \longleftarrow \text{denominator}$$

The **denominator** of a fraction is the total number of equal parts.

The **numerator** of a fraction is the number of parts being counted.

What fraction of each figure is shaded?

	a	b	c

1. 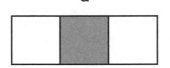      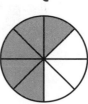

_____   _____   _____

2. 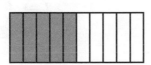   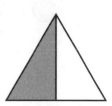

_____   _____   _____

3.   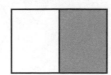   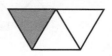

_____   _____   _____

Lesson 7.2 Parts of a Set

Fractions can also be parts of a set.

The denominator is the number of parts in the set. There are 5 pieces in this shape, so the denominator is 5.

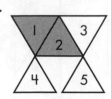

The numerator includes the parts in the set that are shaded. There are 2 parts shaded, so the numerator is 2.

$$\frac{2}{5} \longleftarrow \text{numerator (parts shaded)}$$
$$\phantom{\frac{2}{5}} \longleftarrow \text{denominator (total parts)}$$

Write a fraction for the shaded part of each set.

	a	**b**	**c**

1.      

_____   _____   _____

2.    

_____   _____   _____

3.    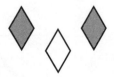   

_____   _____   _____

Lesson 7.3 Comparing Fractions

These fractions have the same denominators.

To find which fraction is larger, look at the numerator.

4 is greater than 3 so 3 < 4.

$\frac{3}{6} \bigcirc< \frac{4}{6}$

Use >, <, or = to compare the fractions.

	a	b	c	d
1.	$\frac{3}{12}$ ___ $\frac{2}{12}$	$\frac{3}{4}$ ___ $\frac{1}{4}$	$\frac{5}{8}$ ___ $\frac{6}{8}$	$\frac{1}{2}$ ___ $\frac{1}{2}$
2.	$\frac{2}{3}$ ___ $\frac{1}{3}$	$\frac{2}{10}$ ___ $\frac{4}{10}$	$\frac{5}{8}$ ___ $\frac{3}{8}$	$\frac{11}{12}$ ___ $\frac{10}{12}$
3.	$\frac{4}{5}$ ___ $\frac{4}{5}$	$\frac{7}{12}$ ___ $\frac{8}{12}$	$\frac{6}{10}$ ___ $\frac{5}{10}$	$\frac{3}{4}$ ___ $\frac{2}{4}$
4.	$\frac{8}{12}$ ___ $\frac{6}{12}$	$\frac{4}{5}$ ___ $\frac{4}{5}$	$\frac{2}{4}$ ___ $\frac{1}{4}$	$\frac{5}{8}$ ___ $\frac{7}{8}$

Lesson 7.4 Finding Equivalent Fractions

$\frac{3}{4}$ To find an equivalent fraction, multiply both the numerator and denominator by the same number.

$\frac{3}{4} = \frac{3 \times 3}{4 \times 3} = \frac{9}{12}$ ← Multiply the numerator by 3.
← Multiply the denominator by 3.

$\frac{3}{4} = \frac{9}{12}$ $\frac{3}{4}$ and $\frac{9}{12}$ are equivalent fractions.

To find an equivalent fraction, multiply the fraction by the number in the circle.

	a	b	c	d
1.	$\frac{3}{4} = $ ___ ③	$\frac{1}{4} = $ ___ ④	$\frac{2}{3} = $ ___ ⑤	$\frac{1}{2} = $ ___ ②
2.	$\frac{1}{3} = $ ___ ⑥	$\frac{3}{12} = $ ___ ②	$\frac{1}{5} = $ ___ ③	$\frac{2}{10} = $ ___ ④
3.	$\frac{5}{7} = $ ___ ②	$\frac{3}{6} = $ ___ ④	$\frac{2}{8} = $ ___ ④	$\frac{1}{6} = $ ___ ⑥
4.	$\frac{1}{3} = $ ___ ⑨	$\frac{2}{3} = $ ___ ⑩	$\frac{2}{5} = $ ___ ⑤	$\frac{1}{8} = $ ___ ②

Use multiplication to find each equivalent fraction.

5.	$\frac{1}{5} = \frac{3}{}$	$\frac{1}{10} = \frac{}{20}$	$\frac{3}{4} = \frac{9}{}$	$\frac{1}{2} = \frac{9}{}$
6.	$\frac{1}{3} = \frac{}{12}$	$\frac{2}{4} = \frac{8}{}$	$\frac{1}{12} = \frac{2}{}$	$\frac{2}{6} = \frac{}{18}$
7.	$\frac{2}{8} = \frac{10}{}$	$\frac{3}{5} = \frac{}{25}$	$\frac{3}{7} = \frac{9}{}$	$\frac{1}{2} = \frac{}{20}$
8.	$\frac{4}{12} = \frac{}{24}$	$\frac{5}{6} = \frac{}{24}$	$\frac{1}{3} = \frac{9}{}$	$\frac{1}{2} = \frac{}{18}$

Lesson 7.4 Finding Equivalent Fractions

$\dfrac{4}{16}$ To find an equivalent fraction, divide both the numerator and denominator by the same number, such as 4.

$\dfrac{4}{16} = \dfrac{4 \div 4}{16 \div 4} = \dfrac{1}{4}$ ⟵ Divide the numerator by 4.
⟵ Divide the denominator by 4.

$\dfrac{4}{16}$ and $\dfrac{1}{4}$ are equivalent fractions.

To find an equivalent fraction, divide the fraction by the number in the circle.

	a	b	c	d
1.	$\dfrac{5}{25} = \underline{\quad}$ ⑤	$\dfrac{12}{24} = \underline{\quad}$ ③	$\dfrac{3}{9} = \underline{\quad}$ ③	$\dfrac{2}{10} = \underline{\quad}$ ②
2.	$\dfrac{6}{36} = \underline{\quad}$ ⑥	$\dfrac{8}{10} = \underline{\quad}$ ②	$\dfrac{4}{20} = \underline{\quad}$ ④	$\dfrac{12}{15} = \underline{\quad}$ ③
3.	$\dfrac{9}{12} = \underline{\quad}$ ③	$\dfrac{14}{16} = \underline{\quad}$ ②	$\dfrac{7}{21} = \underline{\quad}$ ⑦	$\dfrac{2}{18} = \underline{\quad}$ ②
4.	$\dfrac{6}{15} = \underline{\quad}$ ③	$\dfrac{20}{24} = \underline{\quad}$ ④	$\dfrac{2}{4} = \underline{\quad}$ ②	$\dfrac{14}{21} = \underline{\quad}$ ⑦

Use division to find each equivalent fraction.

5.	$\dfrac{24}{30} = \dfrac{}{10}$	$\dfrac{4}{12} = \dfrac{1}{}$	$\dfrac{3}{21} = \dfrac{}{7}$	$\dfrac{5}{20} = \dfrac{}{4}$
6.	$\dfrac{6}{18} = \dfrac{3}{}$	$\dfrac{6}{12} = \dfrac{}{4}$	$\dfrac{10}{25} = \dfrac{2}{}$	$\dfrac{4}{8} = \dfrac{2}{}$
7.	$\dfrac{4}{16} = \dfrac{}{8}$	$\dfrac{4}{18} = \dfrac{}{9}$	$\dfrac{3}{9} = \dfrac{}{3}$	$\dfrac{2}{24} = \dfrac{1}{}$
8.	$\dfrac{3}{21} = \dfrac{1}{}$	$\dfrac{15}{25} = \dfrac{3}{}$	$\dfrac{16}{18} = \dfrac{}{9}$	$\dfrac{4}{12} = \dfrac{}{3}$

Lesson 7.5 Adding Fractions with Like Denominators

$$\frac{2}{8} + \frac{5}{8}$$

Like denominators are the same number.

Add the numerators.

$$\frac{2}{8} + \frac{5}{8} = \frac{2+5}{8} = \frac{7}{8}$$

Write the sum over the common denominator.

Add the fractions.

	a	b	c	d
1.	$\frac{3}{12} + \frac{8}{12} =$ _____	$\frac{2}{5} + \frac{1}{5} =$ _____	$\frac{3}{6} + \frac{2}{6} =$ _____	$\frac{1}{4} + \frac{2}{4} =$ _____
2.	$\frac{1}{10} + \frac{3}{10} =$ _____	$\frac{3}{8} + \frac{2}{8} =$ _____	$\frac{1}{3} + \frac{1}{3} =$ _____	$\frac{2}{7} + \frac{2}{7} =$ _____
3.	$\frac{3}{5} + \frac{1}{5} =$ _____	$\frac{4}{12} + \frac{5}{12} =$ _____	$\frac{3}{10} + \frac{6}{10} =$ _____	$\frac{2}{5} + \frac{2}{5} =$ _____

	a	b	c	d	e
4.	$\frac{3}{8}$ $+\frac{2}{8}$	$\frac{3}{12}$ $+\frac{4}{12}$	$\frac{1}{6}$ $+\frac{1}{6}$	$\frac{2}{6}$ $+\frac{1}{6}$	$\frac{1}{8}$ $+\frac{1}{8}$
5.	$\frac{5}{12}$ $+\frac{3}{12}$	$\frac{3}{7}$ $+\frac{4}{7}$	$\frac{7}{10}$ $+\frac{2}{10}$	$\frac{3}{5}$ $+\frac{1}{5}$	$\frac{8}{12}$ $+\frac{3}{12}$
6.	$\frac{5}{11}$ $+\frac{3}{11}$	$\frac{1}{4}$ $+\frac{1}{4}$	$\frac{1}{2}$ $+\frac{1}{2}$	$\frac{5}{7}$ $+\frac{1}{7}$	$\frac{3}{9}$ $+\frac{1}{9}$

Lesson 7.6 Subtracting Fractions with Like Denominators

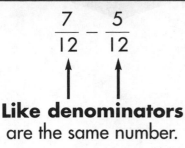

$$\frac{7}{12} - \frac{5}{12}$$

Like denominators are the same number.

Subtract the numerators.

$$\frac{7}{12} - \frac{5}{12} = \frac{7-5}{12} = \frac{2}{12}$$

Write the difference over the common denominator.

The difference between $\frac{7}{12}$ and $\frac{5}{12}$ is $\frac{2}{12}$.

Subtract the fractions.

	a	b	c	d	e
1.	$\frac{11}{12}$ $-\frac{3}{12}$	$\frac{7}{10}$ $-\frac{3}{10}$	$\frac{3}{4}$ $-\frac{1}{4}$	$\frac{6}{7}$ $-\frac{5}{7}$	$\frac{3}{5}$ $-\frac{2}{5}$
2.	$\frac{5}{10}$ $-\frac{3}{10}$	$\frac{8}{12}$ $-\frac{7}{12}$	$\frac{4}{5}$ $-\frac{2}{5}$	$\frac{7}{10}$ $-\frac{4}{10}$	$\frac{5}{8}$ $-\frac{1}{8}$
3.	$\frac{9}{10}$ $-\frac{3}{10}$	$\frac{7}{11}$ $-\frac{5}{11}$	$\frac{8}{9}$ $-\frac{1}{9}$	$\frac{4}{5}$ $-\frac{2}{5}$	$\frac{8}{9}$ $-\frac{6}{9}$

	a	b	c	d
4.	$\frac{5}{7} - \frac{3}{7} =$ ____	$\frac{7}{12} - \frac{3}{12} =$ ____	$\frac{8}{9} - \frac{7}{9} =$ ____	$\frac{12}{12} - \frac{8}{12} =$ ____
5.	$\frac{9}{12} - \frac{7}{12} =$ ____	$\frac{4}{4} - \frac{3}{4} =$ ____	$\frac{9}{10} - \frac{7}{10} =$ ____	$\frac{3}{3} - \frac{1}{3} =$ ____
6.	$\frac{5}{8} - \frac{1}{8} =$ ____	$\frac{6}{7} - \frac{5}{7} =$ ____	$\frac{11}{12} - \frac{8}{12} =$ ____	$\frac{7}{10} - \frac{0}{10} =$ ____

Lesson 7.7 Problem Solving

SHOW YOUR WORK

Solve each problem.

1. Three sisters were told to wash the family car. Paula washed the front $\frac{1}{3}$ and Kelley washed the back $\frac{1}{3}$ of the car. Their sister Mandy didn't show up to wash her part of the car. How much of the car was washed?

   _____ of the car was washed.

2. Autumn has $\frac{3}{4}$ of a bag of apples to feed her horses. If she feeds $\frac{2}{4}$ of the apples to her favorite horse, how much of the bag is left to feed the other horses?

   _____ of a bag of apples is left for the other horses.

3. The library received $\frac{3}{5}$ of its book order. The next day, it received $\frac{1}{5}$ of the order. How much of the book order does the library have?

   The library has _____ of the book order.

4. A group of friends went to the movies. In the lobby, $\frac{4}{8}$ of the group decided to see a comedy and $\frac{2}{8}$ decided to see a mystery. How much of the group wanted to see either a comedy or a mystery?

   _____ of the group wanted to see a comedy or a mystery.

5. In the school cafeteria, $\frac{2}{7}$ of the students were fourth-graders and $\frac{3}{7}$ of the students were fifth-graders. How many students were from the fourth and fifth grades?

   _____ of the students were from the fourth and fifth grades.

6. Koko has $\frac{1}{6}$ of her homework done. If she does another $\frac{4}{6}$ of her homework, how much of it will she have completed?

   Koko will have completed _____ of her homework.

1.	
2.	
3.	
4.	

5.	6.

Lesson 7.8 Understanding Decimals

In 1,324.973 what place value is the 9?

thousands	hundreds	tens	ones	tenths	hundredths	thousandths
1	3	2	4 .	9	7	3

The 9 can be named nine tenths, $\frac{9}{10}$, or 0.9.

Write the place value of the given number.

	a	b	c
1.	3 in $10.03	7 in 7,000.2	5 in 13.5
	_____	_____	_____
2.	2 in $25.75	4 in 5,238.004	8 in 11.8
	_____	_____	_____
3.	1 in $561.07	3 in 0.037	6 in 0.136
	_____	_____	_____

Write the digit that is in the given place value.

	a	b	c	d
4.	432.14 hundred	325.17 tenth	3,214.005 thousandth	25.132 ten
	_____	_____	_____	_____
5.	30.146 hundredth	25.523 thousandth	125.043 tenth	1,325.12 thousand
	_____	_____	_____	_____
6.	100.304 tenth	1.325 hundredth	1.005 thousandth	731.045 one
	_____	_____	_____	_____

Lesson 7.8   Understanding Decimals

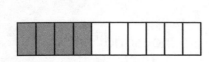

$\frac{4}{10}$ of the box is shaded. $\frac{4}{10}$ = four tenths = 0.4

$\frac{6}{10}$ of the box is unshaded. $\frac{6}{10}$ = six tenths = 0.6

Compare the decimals.

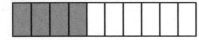

0.6 is greater than 0.4 → 0.6 $>$ 0.4

0.4 is less than 0.6 → 0.4 $<$ 0.6

Write the decimal and fraction for each box.

a	b	c

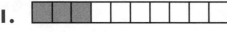 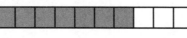 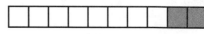

1.

_____ or _____   _____ or _____   _____ or _____

Write the decimal equivalent to the given fraction.

	a	b	c	d

2. $\frac{2}{10}$ = ____ $\frac{6}{10}$ = ____ $\frac{9}{10}$ = ____ $\frac{4}{10}$ = ____

3. $\frac{3}{100}$ = ____ $\frac{4}{1000}$ = ____ $\frac{8}{100}$ = ____ $\frac{5}{1000}$ = ____

Use >, <, or = to compare decimals.

	a	b	c

4.   1.31 ◯ 1.30   0.01 ◯ 1.1   0.008 ◯ 0.009

5.   1.32 ◯ 1.42   1.3 ◯ 1.03   0.66 ◯ .067

Lesson 7.9 Adding Decimals

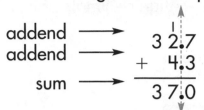

Align decimals points.

addend —→ 3 2.7
addend —→ + 4.3
sum —→ 3 7.0

Align decimal in sum.

To add decimals, first align the decimal point in the addends. Then, add.

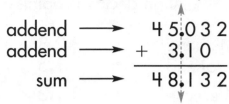

Align decimals points.

addend —→ 4 5.0 3 2
addend —→ + 3.1 0
sum —→ 4 8.1 3 2

Align decimal in sum.

Add.

	a	b	c	d	e
1.	0.3 5 +0.6 5	1.1 +1.3	2.3 +0.4	5.2 +4.6	7.4 +3.5
2.	5.3 +4.9	7.9 +0.7	1 3.3 2 + 5.3 5	1 4.5 0 + 8.6 2	1 0.1 0 + 5.0 5
3.	1.0 5 +0.3 8	8 8.0 3 +1 2.4 8	4 4.1 8 + 2.5 2	3 0.0 3 +1 5.7 4	1 0 2.3 2 + 8 1.3 4
4.	3 1 3.1 7 +2 3 7.4 5	9 3.9 9 +1 7.0 1	5 5 6.7 8 + 5.3 7	8 0.8 0 +3 2.5 5	1 0 0.4 5 +1 0 0.4 5

	a	b	c	d
5.	0.3 1 0.1 0 +0.0 5	1.4 5 0.2 5 +0.1 0	3 2.1 5 8.1 5 + 2.0 5	7 0.0 5 2.1 3 + 0.1 2
6.	1 2 3.7 3 2 4.5 0 + 3.1 2	4 3 4.5 2 + 3 2.0 8	1 7.1 7 1 2.3 6 + 5.0 3	3 2.5 1 3 +1 0.3 1 7

Lesson 7.10 Subtracting Decimals

Align decimals points.

minuend ⟶ 3 2.8
subtrahend ⟶ − 1.5
difference ⟶ 3 1.3

Align decimal in difference.
The difference is 31.3.

> To subtract decimals, first align the decimal points in the minuend and subtrahend. Then, subtract decimals like whole numbers.

Align decimals points.

minuend ⟶ ¹ ¹⁸ 1 4 2.8
subtrahend ⟶ − 1.9
difference ⟶ 1 4 0.9

Align decimal in difference.
The difference is 140.9.

Subtract.

	a	b	c	d	e
1.	7 5.2 − 4.1	4 2.8 −1 2.6	1.2 8 −1.1 3	0.3 2 −0.2 0	1 0.3 − 7.6
2.	5 7 6.2 1 −3 4 1.1 0	8 7.0 9 − 1.1 0	1.3 2 5 −0.1 3 8	6 0.4 7 8 − 7.1 5 2	1 1 7.1 3 − 2 4.0 3
3.	4 3.4 3 +2 1.5 2	3 2.1 7 8 − 0.0 0 9	5.1 9 8 −2.3 8 9	9 8.0 3 −1 7.0 8	0.0 3 2 −0.0 1 3
4.	7.8 1 9 −0.5 0 7	5 2.4 1 9 −2 3.8 1 7	1.9 9 8 −0.7 9 9	0.9 4 5 −0.0 5 2	1 0.1 5 − 8.3 5
5.	3.9 8 7 −1.1 9 3	3 3.9 1 3 −1 5.7 1 5	4.3 5 −1.7 0	3.9 7 8 −1.3 8 2	2 2.8 0 4 −1 7.5 0 4
6.	2.4 1 3 −0.2 0 7	2.9 8 8 −0.7 9 3	5 8.5 8 8 −2 4.9 3 2	7 5.0 5 −1 8.2 5	1 8 3.7 5 −1 4 2.9 4

Lesson 7.11 Adding and Subtracting Money

Align

$$
\begin{array}{r}
\$13.45 \\
-\ 13.32 \\
\hline
\$\ 0.13
\end{array}
$$

Add and subtract money the same way you add and subtract decimals. Align decimal points, and then add or subtract.

Align

$$
\begin{array}{r}
\$1032.35 \\
+\ \ 110.32 \\
\hline
\$1142.67
\end{array}
$$

Add.

	a	b	c	d	e
1.	$13.18 + 7.23	$1.32 + 1.28	72¢ +25¢	35¢ +21¢	$10.42 + 1.38
2.	52¢ 25¢ +10¢	$10.75 5.35 + 2.10	$1325.18 + 867.45	$3.05 + 2.98	75¢ 30¢ +25¢
3.	$596.75 + 13.30	$73.89 + 23.75	$600.15 + 300.17	$5617.52 + 730.61	$105.88 + 92.72

Subtract.

4.	$615.38 – 16.15	98¢ –43¢	$105.17 – 9.37	$5680.18 – 3127.15	85¢ –52¢
5.	$99.99 – 10.98	$29.85 – 18.76	$42.05 – 18.98	33¢ –17¢	$4176.00 – 3042.05
6.	$313.78 – 177.00	$1.19 – 0.32	$27.98 – 18.37	$1413.08 – 852.18	$784.35 – 518.75

Lesson 7.11　Problem Solving

SHOW YOUR WORK

Solve each problem.

1. Jeff wants to buy a vase for $32.75. He only has $25.15. How much does Jeff have to borrow from his brother to buy the vase?

   He has to borrow _____.

2. Booker has to pay his rent. He has $1,252.45 in the bank. His rent is $672.30. How much money will Booker have left in the bank after he pays his rent?

   Booker will have _____ left in the bank.

3. The Thomas triplets want to buy some oranges. Justin has 23 cents, Jarrod has 45 cents, and Jeremy has 52 cents. How much money do the triplets have?

   The triplets have _____.

4. A school lunch costs $1.55. Sean has $2.45. How much money will he have left after buying lunch?

   Sean will have _____.

5. Mr. Wilson just received his bill for $1,867.85 for the wedding dinner party for his daughter. His budget for the dinner was $2,000. How much less did the dinner cost than he expected?

   The dinner cost _____ less than he expected.

6. Opal is buying groceries for dinner. Ravioli costs $3.25, salad costs $1.15, and bread costs $0.35. How much do the groceries cost?

   The groceries cost _____.

1.
2.
3.

4.	5.

6.

Check What You Learned

Fractions, Decimals, and Money

Add or subtract the fractions and decimals.

	a	b	c	d	e
1.	$\dfrac{3}{10}$ $+\dfrac{7}{10}$	$\dfrac{3}{12}$ $+\dfrac{5}{12}$	$\dfrac{5}{10}$ $+\dfrac{2}{10}$	$\dfrac{1}{4}$ $+\dfrac{1}{4}$	$\dfrac{3}{8}$ $+\dfrac{3}{8}$
2.	0.32 $+0.28$	50.05 $+\ 1.78$	13.615 $+\ 1.709$	$\$55.18$ $+\ \ \ 3.92$	$42¢$ $+32¢$
3.	0.1528 $+1.3200$	$\$1294.85$ $+\ \ \ 732.71$	0.005 $+0.008$	0.50 $+0.60$	53.26 $+27.48$
4.	10.932 $+\ \ 9.138$	$\$798.70$ $+\ \ 500.00$	$89¢$ $+75¢$	7.005 $+3.105$	$\$79.15$ $+\ \ 49.48$
5.	500.15 -253.06	$\$137.50$ $-\ \ \ 81.70$	0.052 -0.048	0.158 -0.073	$\$1205.32$ $-\ \ \ 877.81$
6.	$\dfrac{11}{12}$ $-\dfrac{8}{12}$	$\dfrac{8}{9}$ $-\dfrac{5}{9}$	$\dfrac{10}{10}$ $-\dfrac{8}{10}$	$\dfrac{3}{4}$ $-\dfrac{2}{4}$	$\dfrac{7}{8}$ $-\dfrac{4}{8}$

Use >, <, or = to compare decimals or fractions.

	a	b	c	d
7.	$0.32 \bigcirc 0.23$	$\dfrac{11}{12} \bigcirc \dfrac{3}{12}$	$0.4 \bigcirc \dfrac{4}{10}$	$0.015 \bigcirc 0.105$

Check What You Learned

Fractions, Decimals, and Money

Solve each problem.

8. Minato is checking his extra credit points for computer class. If he has received 7.13, 8.73, and 10.52, how many points does he have altogether?

He has _____ points.

9. Ruby ran $\frac{6}{12}$ of a mile on Saturday and $\frac{5}{12}$ of a mile the next day. How far did she run?

She ran _____ of a mile.

10. Afton wants to spend three days at the golf center. The golf center costs $12.00 on Friday, $12.00 on Saturday, and $10.25 on Sunday. How much will it cost to golf over the 3 days?

It will cost _____ to golf over the 3 days.

11. Sabrina wants to buy a pair of tennis shoes for $110.00. However, she only has $78.95. How much money does Sabrina need to save so she can buy the shoes?

Sabrina needs to save _____.

12. After a warm winter, Mr. Hiroshi has $\frac{11}{12}$ of his pile of firewood left. If he uses $\frac{3}{12}$ of the wood tonight for a bonfire, how much of the original pile will be left?

Mr. Hiroshi will have _____ of the original pile left.

13. Matt wanted to buy lunch for his friends. He had $42.00. The lunch bill was $41.90. How much money did Matt have left?

Matt had _____ left.

8.	9.
10.	11.
12.	13.

Check What You Know

Customary Measurement

Complete the following.

	a	**b**
1.	36 inches = _____ yard	8 quarts = _____ gallons
2.	1 cup = _____ ounces	1 mile = _____ yards
3.	2 feet = _____ inches	10 cups = _____ pints
4.	3 feet = _____ yard	8 pints = _____ quarts
5.	10 pints = _____ cups	8 cups = _____ quarts

Measure each line to the nearest half inch.

6. _____ in. ——————   _____ in. ————————

7. _____ in. ————————————   _____ in. ————

Find the perimeter of each shape.

8.

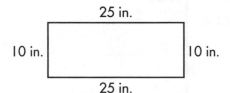

_____ inches

_____ feet

Find the area of each shape.

9.

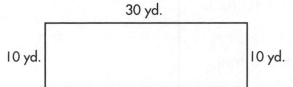

_____ square yards

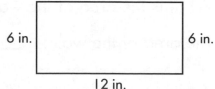

_____ square inches

Check What You Know

SHOW YOUR WORK

Customary Measurement

Solve each problem.

10. Paul is using a 4-quart container to fill a wash tub. If he needs 12 gallons of water to fill the tub, how many times does he need to fill the 4-quart container?

He needs to fill the container _____ times.

11. A worker at the zoo measured the length of an iguana. The iguana measured 72 inches long. How many feet did the iguana measure?

The iguana measured _____ feet.

12. The feed store has a half ton of wood shavings to ship to the horse farm. How many pounds of shavings does the feed store have?

The feed store has _____ pounds of wood shavings.

13. The town of Yarmouth is planning a skateboard park and needs to know the perimeter of the park. The property measures 7 yards by 3 yards by 10 yards by 5 yards. What is the perimeter?

The park's perimeter is _____ yards.

14. The Garcia brothers are painting a wall in their living room. The wall measures 8 feet by 10 feet. What is the area of the wall?

The area of the wall is _____ square feet.

10.

11.

12.

13.

14.

Lesson 8.1 Measuring Inches

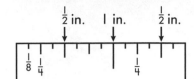

The pipe measures $1\frac{1}{2}$ inches.

The battery measures 1 inch.

Find the length of each object to the nearest $\frac{1}{2}$ inch.

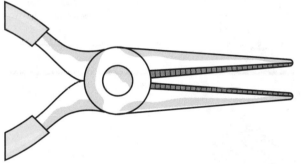

2. _____ in.

1. _____ in.

3. _____ in.

Use a ruler to draw a line segment for each measurement.

4. $\frac{1}{2}$ in.

5. $1\frac{1}{2}$ in.

6. 6 in.

7. $3\frac{1}{2}$ in.

8. 4 in.

9. $5\frac{1}{2}$ in.

Lesson 8.2 Measuring Inches

This button measures $\frac{1}{4}$ inch.

This toothpick measures $1\frac{1}{4}$ inches.

Use a ruler to find the length of each object to the nearest $\frac{1}{4}$ inch.

2. _____ in.

1. _____ in.

3. _____ in. _____

Find the length of each object to the nearest $\frac{1}{8}$ inch.

4. _____ in.

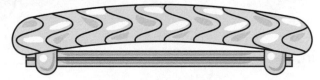

5. _____ in.

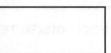

Use a ruler to draw a line for each measurement.

6. $\frac{1}{8}$ in.

7. $4\frac{1}{8}$ in.

8. $\frac{1}{4}$ in.

9. $6\frac{1}{4}$ in.

Lesson 8.3 Units of Length
(inches, feet, yards, and miles)

12 inches = 1 foot (ft.)
3 feet = 1 yard (yd.)
36 inches = 1 yard (yd.)
1,760 yards = 1 mile (mi.)
5,280 feet = 1 mile (mi.)

6 feet = ___ inches

(6 feet × 12 inches)

6 × 12 = 72

6 feet = _72_ inches

_____

72 feet = ___ yards

$$\begin{array}{r} 24 \\ 3\overline{)72} \\ 6 \\ \hline 12 \end{array}$$ 72 feet = _24_ yards

---

Complete the following.

	a	**b**	**c**
1.	5 yd. = _____ ft.	8 ft. = _____ in.	72 yd. = _____ ft.
2.	48 in. = _____ ft.	3 mi. = _____ yd.	24 yd. = _____ in.
3.	3,000 ft. = _____ yd.	24 in. = _____ ft.	2 mi. = _____ ft.
4.	12 in. = _____ ft.	26 yd. = _____ in.	12 ft. = _____ yd.
5.	360 in. = _____ yd.	10 ft. = _____ in.	720 yd. = _____ ft.
6.	7 mi. = _____ yd.	2,400 in. = _____ ft.	324 ft. = _____ yd.
7.	10 mi. = _____ ft.	600 in. = _____ ft.	6 ft. = _____ in.
8.	132 in. = _____ ft.	50 yd. = _____ in.	36 in. = _____ ft.
9.	72 ft. = _____ yd.	36 in. = _____ yd.	3,636 in. = _____ ft.
10.	8 mi. = _____ yd.	48 ft. = _____ yd.	120 in. = _____ ft.

Lesson 8.3 Problem Solving

SHOW YOUR WORK

Solve each problem.

1. Brandy has a curvy slide that is 5 feet long. How many inches long is the slide?

   The slide is _____ inches long.

2. Kristi was competing in the long jump. She jumped 9 feet. How many yards did she jump?

   She jumped _____ yards.

3. The new speedboat measures 25 yards long. How many feet does the speedboat measure?

   The speedboat measures _____ feet.

4. The longest snake is reported to be 36 feet long. How many yards long is the snake?

   The snake is _____ yards long.

5. The hot air balloon is about 4 miles away from its landing strip. How many yards away is the balloon?

   The hot air balloon is _____ yards away.

Estimate your answer and then solve.

6. David's flying disc soared in the wind for 782 feet. About how many yards away did the flying disc go?

   Estimate _____

   The flying disc traveled about _____ yards.

7. The longest human chain was 10,560 feet long. About how many miles was the chain?

   Estimate _____

   The chain was about _____ miles long.

1.	2.
3.	4.
5.	
6.	7.

Lesson 8.4 Liquid Volume
(cups, pints, quarts, and gallons)

Conversion Table	When converting from more to less, multiply.	When converting from less to more, divide.
1 cup (c.) = 8 ounces (oz.)		
1 pint (pt.) = 2 cups (c.)	7 qt. = _____ pt.	16 qt. = _____ gal.
1 quart (qt.) = 2 pints (pt.)	Know: 1 qt. = 2 pt.	Know: 4 qt. = 1 gal.
1 quart (qt.) = 4 cups (c.)	$7 \times 2 = 14$	$16 \div 4 = 4$
1 gallon (gal.) = 4 quarts (qt.)	7 qt. = 14 pt.	16 qt. = 4 gal.
1 gallon (gal.) = 8 pints (pt.)		
1 gallon (gal.) = 16 cups (c.)		

Complete the following.

	a	b	c
1.	2 gal. = _____ qt.	4 pt. = _____ qt.	12 c. = _____ pt.
2.	24 qt. = _____ gal.	16 oz. = _____ c.	10 qt. = _____ pt.
3.	14 pt. = _____ qt.	28 qt. = _____ gal.	14 pt. = _____ c.
4.	48 c. = _____ pt.	32 oz. = _____ c.	14 c. = _____ pt.
5.	10 gal. = _____ qt.	30 pt. = _____ c.	18 c. = _____ pt.
6.	12 gal. = _____ qt.	22 pt. = _____ qt.	64 oz. = _____ c.
7.	30 pt. = _____ qt.	20 c. = _____ oz.	40 qt. = _____ gal.
8.	18 c. = _____ pt.	44 pt. = _____ c.	80 qt. = _____ pt.
9.	150 qt. = _____ pt.	200 c. = _____ pt.	40 c. = _____ oz.
10.	88 oz. = _____ c.	16 qt. = _____ gal.	50 qt. = _____ pt.

Lesson 8.5 Weight (ounces, pounds, and tons)

Conversion Table

one-half pound (lb.) = 8 ounces (oz.)

1 pound (lb.) = 16 ounces (oz.)

one-half ton (T.) = 1,000 pounds (lb.)

1 ton (T.) = 2,000 pounds (lb.)

When converting from more to less, multiply.

5 lb. = _____ oz.

Know:

  1 lb. = 16 oz.

5 × 16 = 80

5 lb. = 80 oz.

When converting from less to more, divide.

6,000 lb. = _____ T.

Know:

  2,000 lb. = 1 T.

6,000 ÷ 2,000 = 3

6,000 lb. = 3 T.

Complete the following.

	a	b	c
1.	32 oz. = _____ lb.	6,000 lb. = _____ T.	4 T. = _____ lb.
2.	40 lb. = _____ oz.	64 oz. = _____ lb.	2,4000 lb. = _____ T.
3.	1,000 lb. = _____ T.	8 oz. = _____ lb.	1,8000 lb. = _____ T.
4.	8 lb. = _____ oz.	12 lb. = _____ oz.	1,0000 lb. = _____ T.

	Tons	Pounds	Ounces
5.	5	_____	160,000
6.	_____	4,000	64,000
7.	3	6,000	_____
8.	4	8,000	_____
9.	_____	2,000	32,000
10.	6	12,000	_____
11.	10	_____	320,000

Lesson 8.6 Problem Solving

SHOW YOUR WORK

Solve each problem.

1. The cooks made 120 quarts of lemonade for the summer concerts. How many gallons did they make?

   They made _____ gallons of lemonade.

2. A large ship was being loaded with 20 tons of grain. How many pounds did the grain weigh?

   The grain weighed _____ pounds.

3. The largest wheel of cheese in Malhman City weighs 985 pounds. How many ounces does the cheese weigh?

   The cheese weighs _____ ounces.

4. Tito and Jack pumped 75 gallons of water out of their flooded basement. How many quarts did they pump out of their basement?

   They pumped _____ quarts of water out of their basement.

5. The airport baggage trailer carried 3 tons of luggage this week. How many pounds of luggage did the trailer carry?

   The trailer carried _____ pounds of luggage.

6. The recipe stated that 12 quarts of water needed to be added to the punch. How many gallons of water did the recipe call for?

   The recipe called for _____ gallons of water.

1.	2.
3.	**4.**
5.	**6.**

Lesson 8.7   Measuring Perimeter

Perimeter is the distance around a shape.

To calculate perimeter, add together the lengths of all the sides.

Perimeter = 17 in. + 10 in. + 17 in. + 10 in.

Perimeter = 54 in.

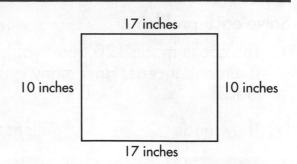

Find the perimeter of each shape.

	a	b	c

1.

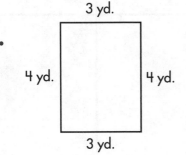

3 yd.
4 yd.   4 yd.
3 yd.
___ yd.

5 ft.
10 ft.   10 ft.
5 ft.
___ ft.

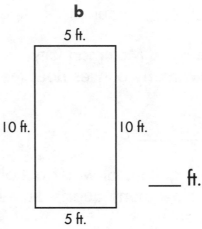
13 in.   13 in.
2 in.
___ in.

2.

75 yd.
50 yd.
100 yd.
___ yd.

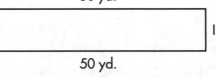
50 yd.
10 yd.   10 yd.
50 yd.
___ yd.

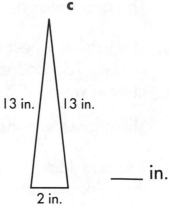
25 ft.
13 ft.
17 ft.
___ ft.

3.

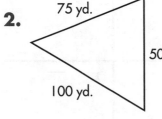
5 ft.
15 ft.
15 ft.
7 ft.
___ ft.

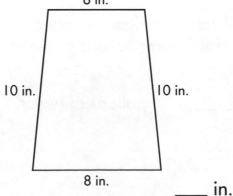
6 in.
10 in.   10 in.
8 in.
___ in.

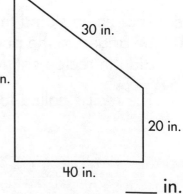
30 in.
60 in.
20 in.
40 in.
___ in.

Lesson 8.8   Measuring Area

To find the area of a square or rectangle, multiply length by width.

100 ft. × 20 ft. = 2,000 sq. ft.

The product is written as 2,000 square feet.

100 ft. (length)

20 ft. (width)

Find the area of each shape.

	a	b	c	d

1.

15 in.

12 in.

_____ sq. in.

12 ft.

12 ft.

_____ sq. ft.

12 ft.

11 ft.

_____ sq. ft.

35 in.

50 in.

_____ sq. in.

	a	b	c

2.

10 yd.

25 yd.

_____ sq. yd.

5 in.

8 in.

_____ sq. in.

12 yd.

40 yd.

_____ sq. yd.

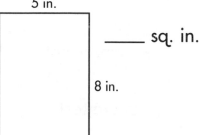

	a	b

3.

23 yd.

8 yd.

_____ sq. yd.

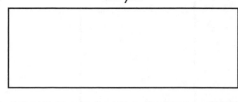

20 ft.

4 ft.

_____ sq. ft.

Lesson 8.9 Problem Solving

SHOW YOUR WORK

Solve each problem.

1. John cleared a vacant lot to plant a garden. The lot measured 35 by 15 feet. What is the perimeter of the garden lot?

   The perimeter of the lot is _____ feet.

2. Freda is putting carpet down in a room that measures 20 feet long by 30 feet wide. What is the area of the room?

   The area is _____ square feet.

3. The zoo is building a new hippo pool that will measure 55 by 75 feet. What is the area of the pool?

   The area is _____ square feet.

4. Gabriel built a cage for his tropical birds. The cage measures 14 feet by 12 feet. What is the perimeter of the cage?

   The perimeter of the cage is _____ feet.

5. The Foster's deck was almost finished. Each side of the square deck was 25 feet long. What was the area of the deck?

   The area was _____ square feet.

6. The length of the walking track is 103 feet and the width is 50 feet. What is the perimeter of the track?

   The perimeter is _____ feet.

7. The college donated land for a park. The land is 750 feet long and 25 feet wide. What is the area of the land?

   The area is _____ square feet.

1.	
2.	
3.	
4.	
5.	
6.	7.

Check What You Learned

Customary Measurement

Find the length of each line.

           a   **b**

1. _____ in. _____   _____ in. _____

2. _____ in. ———   _____ in. ————————

Complete the following.

           a   **b**   **c**

3. 4 ft. = _____ in.   5 lb. = _____ oz.   2 T. = _____ lb.

4. 4 qt. = _____ gal.   72 oz. = _____ c.   15 yd. = _____ ft.

5. 5,280 yd. = _____ mi.   17 pt. = _____ c.   80 oz. = _____ lb.

Find the perimeter of each shape.

                       a   **b**

6.

13 ft.   20 yd.

9 ft.   9 ft.   15 yd.   10 yd.

                  _____ ft.

13 ft.   _____ yd.

Find the area of each shape.

7.

10 ft.   15 in.

30 ft.   15 in.

       _____ sq. ft.   _____ sq. in.

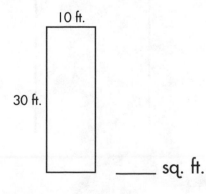
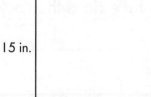

Check What You Learned

Customary Measurement

Solve each problem.

8. The new refrigerator holds 16 quarts of juice. How many gallons does the refrigerator hold?

   The refrigerator holds _____ gallons.

9. The local dairy sold 60 pints of chocolate milk to the fourth grade class. How many cups of milk did the dairy sell to the class?

   The dairy sold _____ cups of milk to the class.

10. At the store, a container of ice cream weighs 32 ounces. How many pounds does the container of ice cream weigh?

    The container of ice cream weighs _____ pounds.

11. There is a 50-pound limit on airline baggage. How many ounces is the limit?

    The limit is _____ ounces.

12. Kara walks $1\frac{1}{2}$ miles to school every day. How many feet does she walk to school?

    She walks _____ feet.

13. The picnic cooler holds 10 pounds of ice. How many ounces of ice does the cooler hold?

    The cooler holds _____ ounces.

8.	9.
10.	**11.**
12.	**13.**

CHAPTER 8 POSTTEST

Check What You Know

Metric Measurement

Complete the following.

	a	b
1.	5 km = _____ m	60,000 mL = _____ L
2.	6 m = _____ cm	32 kg = _____ g
3.	72 cm = _____ mm	19 L = _____ mL
4.	1 g = _____ mg	100 cm = _____ m
5.	25 kg = _____ g	65 cm = _____ mm
6.	17 L = _____ mL	5,200 cm = _____ m
7.	7,000 mg = _____ g	25 km = _____ m
8.	200 mm = _____ cm	9,000 mL = _____ L

Find the length of each rectangle to the nearest centimeter.

9. _____ cm   _____ cm

10. _____ cm   _____ cm

Find the length of one side of each square to the nearest millimeter.

11. _____ mm   _____ mm

12. _____ mm   _____ mm

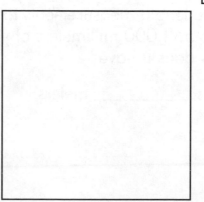

Check What You Know

Metric Measurement

SHOW YOUR WORK

Solve each problem.

13. A hiking trail is 35 kilometers long. The trail is how many meters long?

The hiking trail is _____ meters long.

14. The ham in the store weighs 1 kilogram. How many grams does the ham weigh?

The ham weighs _____ grams.

15. Shawna ordered liters of ginger ale for a party, but she found that it only comes in milliliters. If she orders 30,000 milliliters, how many liters will she have?

She will have _____ liters.

16. The science experiment requires the students to measure the chemicals in grams. If there are 52,000 milligrams of chemicals, how many grams of chemicals do they have?

They have _____ grams of chemicals.

17. When a store orders yarn, it orders the lengths in millimeters. For the store to sell the yarn, it needs to convert the length measurements to meters. If the store has 564,000 millimeters of yarn, how many meters does it have?

The store has _____ meters.

13.	14.

15.

16.

17.

Lesson 9.1 Measuring in Centimeters

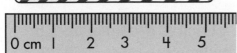

The straw is about __5__ centimeters (cm) long.

The stamp is about __2__ centimeters long.

Use a ruler and pencil to finish the shape. Find the length of the missing side in centimeters.

a   **b**

1. _____ cm   _____ cm

2. _____ cm   _____ cm

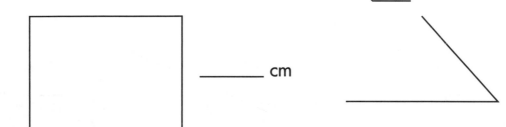

Find the length of each line segment to the nearest centimeter.

3. _____ cm   _____ cm

4. _____ cm   _____ cm

Use a ruler to draw a line segment for each measurement.

5. 2 centimeters

6. 6 centimeters

7. 12 centimeters

8. 7 centimeters

Lesson 9.2 Measuring in Millimeters

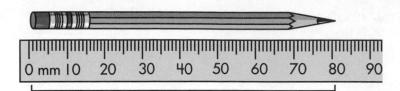

The pencil is 8 centimeters or 80 millimeters long.

80 millimeters or 8 centimeters

I centimeter (cm) = 10 millimeters (mm)
I cm = 10 mm

Use a ruler and pencil to finish the shape. Find the length of the missing side in millimeters.

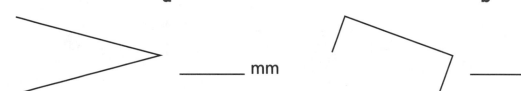

| | a | b |

1. _____ mm   _____ mm

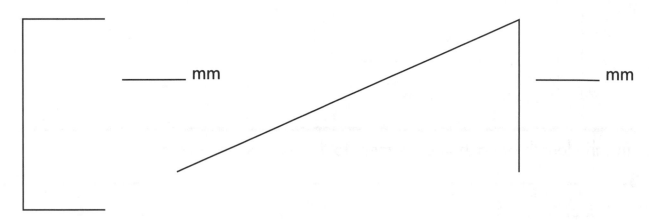

2. _____ mm   _____ mm

Complete the following.

| | a | b |

3. 7 cm = _____ mm   2 cm = _____ mm

4. 5 cm = _____ mm   60 mm = _____ cm

5. 90 mm = _____ cm   11 cm = _____ mm

6. 100 mm = _____ cm   25 cm = _____ mm

Lesson 9.3 Meters and Kilometers

100 centimeters (cm) = 1 meter (m)	1,000 meters (m) = 1 kilometer (km)
100 cm = 1 m	1,000 m = 1 km

Find the length of each of the following objects around your home to the nearest meter.

	Object	Length (m)
1.	width of TV screen	_____ m
2.	height of stove	_____ m
3.	height of computer	_____ m
4.	width of your bed	_____ m
5.	height of TV	_____ m
6.	your height	_____ m
7.	width of a window	_____ m

Complete the following.

	a	**b**
8.	600 cm = _____ m	9,000 m = _____ km
9.	7 m = _____ cm	10,000 m = _____ km
10.	7 km = _____ m	23 km = _____ m
11.	8 m = _____ cm	32 m = _____ cm
12.	2 km = _____ m	14 m = _____ cm

Lesson 9.4 Units of Length (millimeters, centimeters, meters, and kilometers)

7 cm = ___ mm	3 m = ___ mm	32 m = ___ cm	15 km = ___ m
1 cm = 10 mm	1 m = 1,000 mm	1 m = 100 cm	1 km = 1,000 m
1 10 ×7 × 7 7 70	1 1000 ×3 × 3 3 3000	1 100 ×32 × 32 32 3200	1 1000 ×15 × 15 15 15000
7 cm = 70 mm	3 m = 3,000 mm	32 m = 3,200 cm	15 km = 15,000 m

Complete the following.

a   b

1. 4 m = _____ cm   25 m = _____ mm

2. 21 km = _____ m   25 cm = _____ mm

3. 33 m = _____ cm   14 km = _____ m

4. 15 m = _____ cm   47 m = _____ mm

5. 5 km = _____ m   84 cm = _____ mm

6. 75 m = _____ cm   72 m = _____ cm

7. 10 km = _____ m   66 m = _____ mm

8. 21 cm = _____ mm   19 km = _____ m

Spectrum Math
Grade 4
122

Chapter 9, Lesson 4
Metric Measurement

Lesson 9.5 Measuring Perimeter

Perimeter is the distance around a shape.

The perimeter of this shape would be

5 m + 10 m + 7 m + 10 m = 32 m

The perimeter is __32 m__.

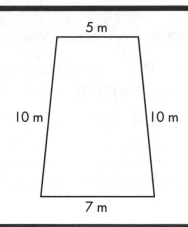

Find the perimeter of each shape.

a   b   c

1.

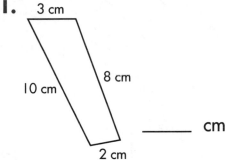

_____ cm

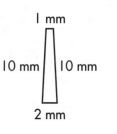

_____ mm

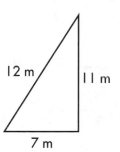

_____ m

2.

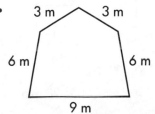

_____ m

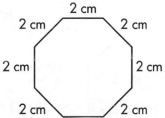

_____ cm

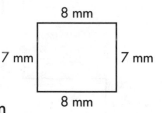

_____ mm

Measure the length of each side in centimeters or millimeters. Then, find the perimeter.

a   b

3.

perimeter = _____ cm

perimeter = _____ cm

4.

perimeter = _____ mm

perimeter = _____ mm

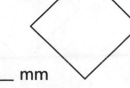

Lesson 9.6 Measuring Area

Area is the measurement of a surface.

To find the area of a square or a rectangle, multiply length by width.

The area of this rectangle is 32 square millimeters.

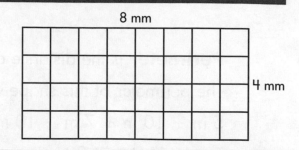

8 mm

4 mm

Find the area of each square or rectangle.

	a	b	c

1.

30 mm
2 mm

_____ sq. mm

4 m

4 m

_____ sq. m

2 cm

7 cm

_____ sq. cm

2.

15 m

7 m

_____ sq. m

10 cm

7 cm

_____ sq. cm

3 mm

18 mm

_____ sq. mm

3.

23 m

12 m

_____ sq. m

3 cm

17 cm

_____ sq. cm

4 mm

20 mm

_____ sq. mm

4.

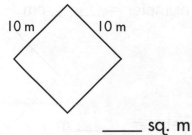

10 m   10 m

_____ sq. m

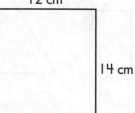

12 cm

14 cm

_____ sq. cm

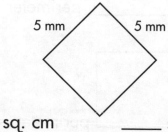

5 mm   5 mm

_____ sq. mm

Lesson 9.7 Liquid Volume (milliliters)

1 liter (L) = 1,000 milliliters (mL)
1 L = 1,000 mL

4 liters = ___ milliliters

1 liter = 1,000 milliliters

$$
\begin{array}{cc}
1 & 1000 \\
\times 4 & \times\ \ \ \ 4 \\
\hline
4 & 4000
\end{array}
$$

4 liters = 4,000 milliliters

Complete the following.

	a	b	c
1.	3 L = _____ mL	12 L = _____ mL	2 L = _____ mL
2.	75 L = _____ mL	10 L = _____ mL	50 L = _____ mL
3.	13 L = _____ mL	78 L = _____ mL	8 L = _____ mL

SHOW YOUR WORK

Solve each problem.

4. A pool for the dogs needs 75 liters of water. How many milliliters of water are needed?

_____ milliliters of water are needed.

5. Mitchell is making the punch and needs 7,000 milliliters of pineapple juice. How many liters of juice does he need?

He needs _____ liters of juice.

6. The pitcher holds 2 milliliters. How many pitchers does Jose need to fill a 24-milliliter punch bowl?

Jose needs _____ pitchers to fill the bowl.

4.

5.   **6.**

Lesson 9.8 Weight (milligrams, grams, and kilograms)

13 g = ___ mg 1 g = 1,000 mg ↓ ↓ 1 1 0 0 0 × 1 3 × 1 3 ——— ————— 1 3 1 3 0 0 0 ↓ ↓ 13 g = 13,000 g	1 gram (g) = 1,000 milligrams (mg) 1 g = 1,000 mg	55 kg = ___ g 1 kg = 1,000 g ↓ ↓ 1 1 0 0 0 × 5 5 × 5 5 ——— ————— 5 5 5 5 0 0 0 ↓ ↓ 55 kg = 55,000 g	1,000 grams (g) = 1 kilogram (kg) 1,000 g = 1 kg

Complete the following.

	a	**b**	**c**
1.	6 kg = _____ g	32 g = _____ mg	45 kg = _____ g
2.	10 g = _____ mg	42 kg = _____ g	9 g = _____ mg
3.	105 g = _____ mg	37 g = _____ mg	12 kg = _____ g
4.	183 kg = _____ g	18 g = _____ mg	119 kg = _____ g

SHOW YOUR WORK

Solve each problem.

5. The bags Jon carries weigh 45,000 mg each. How many grams does each bag weigh?

Each bag weighs _____ grams.

6. Teresa's vitamins contain 7,000 milligrams of vitamin E. How many grams of vitamin E does Teresa take in each vitamin?

Teresa takes _____ grams.

5.

6.

Check What You Learned

Metric Measurement

Complete the following.

	a	**b**
1.	600 mm = _____ cm	2,050 cm = _____ mm
2.	13 cm = _____ mm	4 m = _____ cm
3.	37 km = _____ m	15 L = _____ mL
4.	44 g = _____ mg	9 kg = _____ g
5.	95 m = _____ cm	220 cm = _____ mm
6.	5,000 m = _____ km	76 m = _____ cm
7.	56 m = _____ cm	232 km = _____ m
8.	865 cm = _____ mm	45 L = _____ mL
9.	267 g = _____ mg	26 kg = _____ g
10.	2 L = _____ mL	15 cm = _____ mm
11.	22 m = _____ mm	67 km = _____ m
12.	300 cm = _____ m	3,000 m = _____ km

Find the perimeter of each shape.

13.

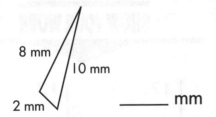

_____ mm

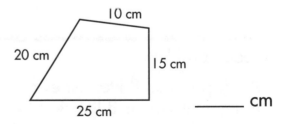

_____ cm

14.

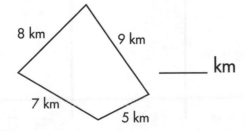

_____ km

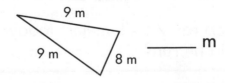

_____ m

Check What You Learned

Metric Measurement

Find the area of each shape.

a   **b**

15.

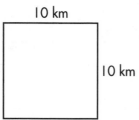

10 km

10 km

area = _____ square kilometers

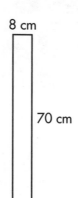

8 cm

70 cm

area = _____ square centimeters

16.

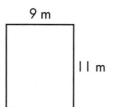

9 m

11 m

area = _____ square meters

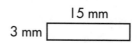

15 mm

3 mm

area = _____ square millimeters

SHOW YOUR WORK

Solve each problem.

17. A recipe listed 8 liters of evaporated milk. How many milliliters is 8 liters?

8 liters is _____ milliliters of milk.

18. Bob ran 75 kilometers today. How many meters did he run?

Bob ran _____ meters.

17.   **18.**

NAME _____

 # Check What You Know

Graphs and Probability

Use the line graph to answer questions 1–3.

1. What day of the week did Alicia spend the most money?

Alicia spent the most money on

_____ .

2. About how much money did Alicia spend on Tuesday?

Alicia spent about _____ on Tuesday.

3. What trend does the graph show from Sunday to Saturday?

From Sunday to Saturday, the amount Alicia spends _____ each day.

Use the bar graph to answer each question.

4. About how many pounds of celery were sold at Miller's Market?

About _____ pounds of celery were sold.

5. What is the difference between the amount of corn sold and the amount of potatoes sold?

About _____ pounds more corn was sold than potatoes.

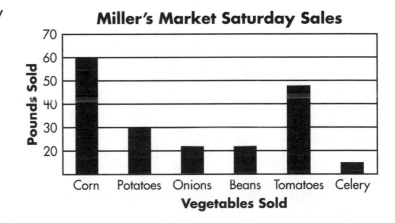

Circle *true* or *false* under each statement.

6. The tomatoes, corn, and beans sold add up to about 130 pounds.

True   False

7. Miller's Market sold over 190 pounds of vegetables on Saturday.

True   False

8. Based on weight, the top three vegetables sold were corn, potatoes, and tomatoes.

True   False

Check What You Know

Graphs and Probability

Find the probability of each event.

9. What is the probability of spinning an **8** on this wheel?

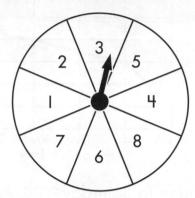

The probability of spinning an 8 is _____.

10. What is the probability of spinning an **i** on this wheel?

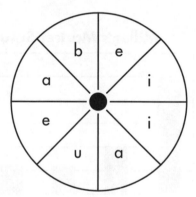

The probability of spinning an **i** is _____.

SHOW YOUR WORK

Solve the problem.

11. In a bag of 15 candy bars, there are 5 chocolate, 5 vanilla, and 5 strawberry candy bars. What is the probability of picking out a vanilla candy bar?

The probability of picking out a vanilla candy bar

is _____.

11.

Lesson 10.1   Reading Bar Graphs

A **bar graph** is used to compare data. The data is shown on the graph with bars.

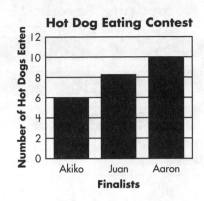

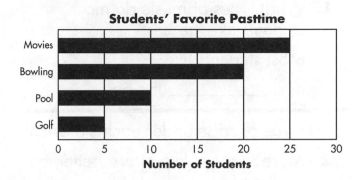

This bar graph compares the amount of hot dogs eaten by the finalists. The bar for Aaron is the longest because Aaron ate the most hot dogs (10).

This bar graph compares students' favorite pasttimes. The bar for movies is the longest because 25 students like to go to the movies.

Read each graph and answer the questions.

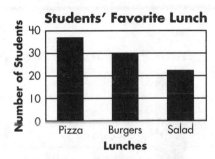

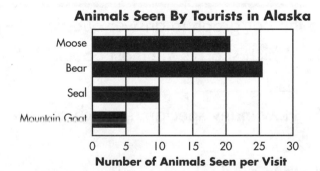

1. What is the favorite lunch shown by the graph?

_____ is the favorite lunch.

Circle *true* or *false* under each statement.

2. Students like to eat more salads than burgers.

True   False

3. Thirty students like to eat burgers.

True   False

4. Look at the bar graph. What is the animal most often seen in Alaska by tourists?

The _____ is the animal most often seen.

5. Moose and mountain goats are not seen very often.

True   False

6. Moose and bears are seen the most.

True   False

Lesson 10.1   Problem Solving

Use the bar graph to answer questions 1–4.

1. What types of music do most students like the best?

   Most students like _____

   and _____ the best.

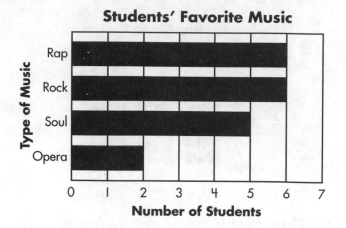

Students' Favorite Music

Circle *true* or *false* under each statement.

2. More students like opera better than soul music.

   True   False

3. Soul is the favorite type of music.

   True   False

4. The least favorite type of music is opera.

   True   False

Use the bar graph to answer questions 5–10.

5. Which sport is the most popular?

   _____

6. How many spectators watch soccer?

   _____

7. What is the least watched sport?

   _____

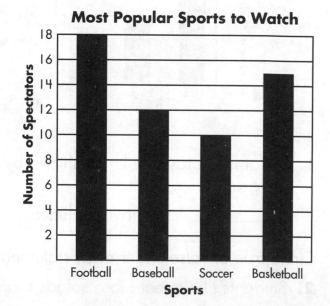

Most Popular Sports to Watch

Circle *true* or *false* under each statement.

8. Baseball is as popular as basketball.

   True   False

9. Twelve spectators enjoy watching baseball.

   True   False

10. About 3 more spectators watch football than basketball.

    True   False

Lesson 10.2 Reading Line Graphs

A **line graph** shows gradual changes over time. The information is shown on the graph by a line that connects points on the graph.

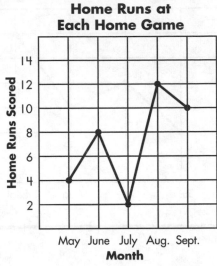

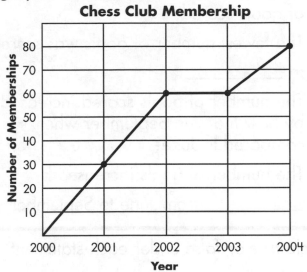

This line graph shows the number of home runs at home games in one season.

This line graph shows how a chess club membership has grown over a period of years.

Study each graph and answer the questions.

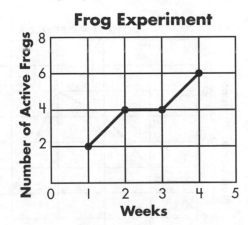

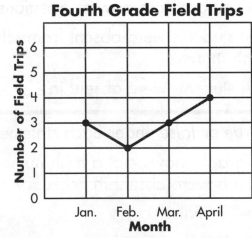

1. In what week were the most frogs active? _____

2. Between which 2 weeks was there no change in the number of active frogs?

_____

3. Fourth graders had the fewest field trips in what month? _____

4. How many field trips did fourth graders have in January?

_____

Lesson 10.2   Problem Solving

Use the line graph to answer questions 1–4.

1. In which month was the fewest number of goals scored?

The fewest number of goals was scored

in _____ .

2. The number of goals scored increased by how many in September when compared to June?

The number of goals increased by

_____ from June to September.

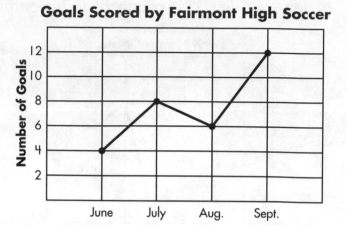

Goals Scored by Fairmont High Soccer

Circle *true* or *false* under each statement.

3. Fairmont shows a steady increase in the number of goals scored from month to month.

True   False

4. August was the low point in the number of goals scored.

True   False

Use the line graph to answer questions 5–9.

5. Most students were absent from school in which month?

Most students were absent in _____ .

Circle *true* or *false* under each statement.

6. The graph shows that a high number of students were absent in February.

True   False

7. There is a decrease in absences around the December holidays.

True   False

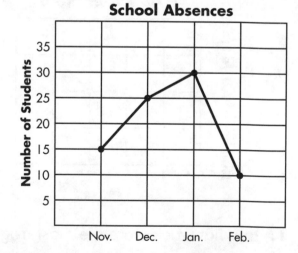

School Absences

8. Five more students were absent in February than in November.

True   False

9. Ten fewer students were absent in November than in December.

True   False

Lesson 10.3 Probability

Probability is the chance of an event occurring.

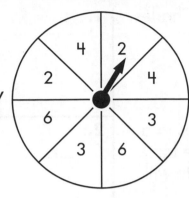

Use a fraction to describe the probability of getting a **6** on a spin.

There are eight possible outcomes of a spin: 2, 4, 2, 4, 3, 6, 3, and 6. Use the number of outcomes as the denominator of the fraction: $\frac{?}{8}$.

There are 2 ways to spin a **6**. Use this number as the numerator of the fraction: $\frac{2}{8}$.

The probability of spinning a **6** is $\frac{2}{8}$.

Find the probability of each event.

1. What is the probability of spinning a **1** on this wheel?

The probability of spinning a **1** is _____.

2. What is the probability of spinning a **4** on this wheel?

The probability of spinning a **4** is _____.

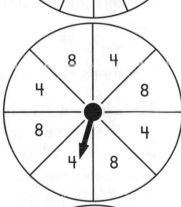

3. What is the probability of spinning a **1** on this wheel?

The probability of spinning a **1** is _____.

4. What is the probability of spinning a **5** on this wheel?

The probability of spinning a **5** is _____.

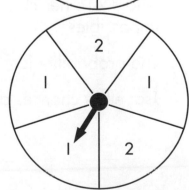

Lesson 10.3   Problem Solving

Solve each problem.

1. In a raffle, there are 35 chances to win. If Charles buys 10 chances, what is the probability that Charles will win?

The probability is _____.

2. All members of the gym class put their names in a jar. The coach selected 4 teams of equal size for dodgeball. What is the probability that Dante will get onto his friend's team?

The probability is _____.

3. Heather and 14 friends rushed the table to get a slice of their favorite cheesecake. There are 3 slices left. Assume that all the girls have an equal chance of getting a piece of cake. What is the probability that Heather might get a slice of cheesecake? What is her chance of getting a slice: certain, likely, unlikely, or impossible?

The probability is _____.

Heather's chances are _____.

4. Isabella put 100 marbles in a jar and shook the jar. There are 4 colors of marbles. There are 25 of each color. What is the probability that Isabella will pick a marble out of the jar that is in her favorite color? Are her chances certain, likely, unlikely, or impossible?

The probability is _____.

Isabella's chances are _____.

1.

2.

3.

4.

Check What You Learned

Graphs and Probability

Use the line graph to answer questions 1–4.

1. On which Sunday was the smallest dollar amount collected?

The smallest dollar amount was collected on the _____ Sunday.

2. How much money was collected on the fourth Sunday?

$_____ was collected on the fourth Sunday.

Circle *true* or *false* under each statement.

3. The best time to collect dues is at the beginning of the month.

True   False

4. Over $12 was collected in the month of June.

True   False

Dues Collected for Neighborhood Newsletter

CHAPTER 10 POSTTEST

Use the bar graph to answer questions 5–8.

5. Which type of pet had the best sales in August?

_____ had the best sales in August.

Circle *true* or *false* under each statement.

6. The pet store sold 5 more gerbils than puppies in August.

True   False

7. The pet store sold fewer puppies than kittens or gerbils. But there was not much difference in the sales of gerbils, puppies, and kittens.

True   False

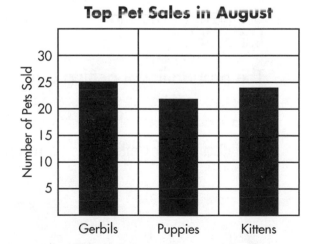

Top Pet Sales in August

8. The pet store sold almost as many kittens as puppies in August.

True   False

Check What You Learned

SHOW YOUR WORK

Graphs and Probability

Solve each problem.

9. What is the probability of spinning a **3**?

   The probability of spinning

   a **3** is _____.

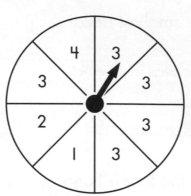

9.

10. What is the probability of spinning a **1**?

    The probability of spinning a **1** is _____.

10.

11.

11. What is the probability of spinning a **5**?

    The probability of spinning a **5** is _____.

12. Chaz has a bag of marbles in 7 different colors. If there are 7 marbles in the bag, what is the probability of getting a red marble? Is the chance of getting a red marble certain, unlikely, likely, or impossible?

    The probability of getting a red marble is

    _____.

    The chance of getting a red marble is _____.

12.

Check What You Know

Geometry

Identify each plane figure.

    a   **b**   **c**   **d**

1.

_____   _____   _____   _____

Identify each solid figure as a cube, cylinder, rectangular prism, square pyramid, or sphere.

    a   **b**   **c**   **d**

2.    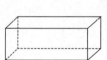   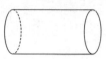

_____   _____   _____   _____

Identify how each figure has been moved by writing slide, flip, or turn.

    a   **b**   **c**

3.   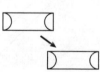

_____   _____   _____

Identify each pair of plane figures as congruent or not congruent.

    a   **b**   **c**

4. 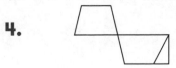   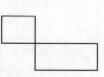

_____   _____   _____

CHAPTER 11 PRETEST

Check What You Know

Geometry

Identify these geometric figures: point, line, line segment, ray, vertex.

         a   **b**   **c**

5. 

_____ _____ _____

6.

_____ _____

Identify each angle as right, acute, or obtuse.

7.      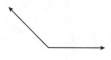

_____ _____ _____

Identify each pair of lines as parallel or perpendicular.

8.

_____ _____ _____

9. Plot the ordered pairs on the graph.

(0, 2) (1, 1) (3, 0)

10. Identify the location of each ordered pair on the graph.

A _____

B _____

C _____

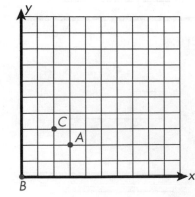

Lesson 11.1 Plane Figures

Polygons are closed plane figures. They have 3 or more straight sides.

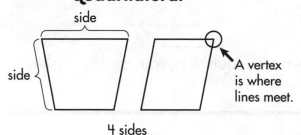

quadrilateral

side

side

A vertex is where lines meet.

4 sides

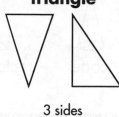

triangle

3 sides

pentagon

5 sides

hexagon

6 sides

heptagon

7 sides

octagon

8 sides

nonagon

9 sides

Identify each plane figure as a triangle, quadrilateral, pentagon, hexagon, heptagon, octagon, or nonagon.

	a	b	c
1.	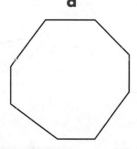	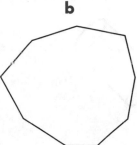	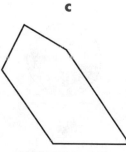
	_____	_____	_____
2.	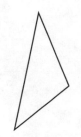		
	_____	_____	_____

Lesson 11.2 Solid Figures

Solid figures have 3 dimensions and they can appear hollow or solid.

  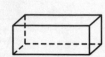 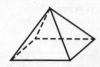

| cube | cylinder | cone | rectangular prism | square pyramid | sphere |

Identify these plane and solid figures.

	a	**b**	**c**	**d**
1.		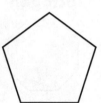	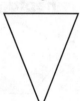	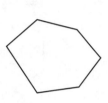
	_____	_____	_____	_____
2.		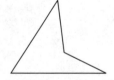		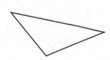
	_____	_____	_____	_____
3.		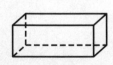	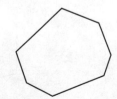	
	_____	_____	_____	_____

Lesson 11.3 Congruent Figures

Congruence refers to two shapes of exactly the same size and shape.

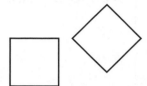

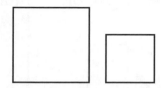

These 2 shapes are **congruent** because they are exactly the same size and exactly the same shape.

These 2 shapes are **not congruent.** They are exactly the same shape, but they are not exactly the same size.

Identify each pair of plane figures as congruent or not congruent.

	a	**b**	**c**

1.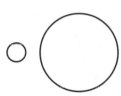

_____   _____   _____

2.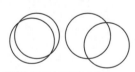

_____   _____   _____

3.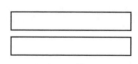

_____   _____   _____

4.

_____   _____   _____

Lesson 11.4   Slides, Flips, and Turns

Slide a figure to move it up, down, left, right, or diagonally.

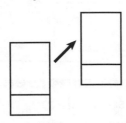

Flip a figure to create a mirror image.

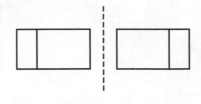

Turn a figure to rotate it around a point.

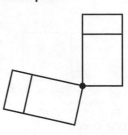

Identify how each figure has been moved by writing slide, flip, or turn.

	a	b	c

1.

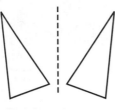      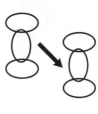

_____   _____   _____

2.

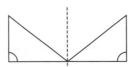   _____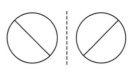

_____   _____   _____

3.

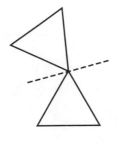   _____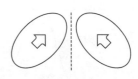

_____   _____   _____

Lesson 11.5 Points, Lines, and Rays

A **point** is an exact location in space. It has no length or width.	A **line** goes on infinitely in both directions. It has no endpoints.	A **line segment** is part of a line. It has two endpoints and includes all points between those endpoints.	A **ray** is part of a line. It has one endpoint and continues on and on in one direction.	A **vertex** is an endpoint formed from two rays sharing a common endpoint.

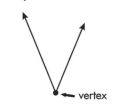

Identify the following figures.

	a	b	c	d
1.			•	
	_____	_____	_____	_____
2.				
	_____	_____	_____	_____

Compare the following figures with examples at the top of the page. Complete the figures.

3. _____

line   ray   line segment   vertex

Draw these figures.

	a	b	c	d	e
4.	line segment	ray	vertex	point	line
	_____	_____	_____	_____	_____

Lesson 11.6 Identifying Angles

An **angle** consists of two rays with the same vertex.

| **Right angle** | **Acute angle**
(smaller than a right angle) | **Obtuse angle**
(larger than a right angle) |

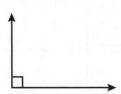 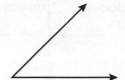 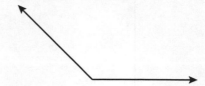

Identify each angle as right, acute, obtuse.

	a	b	c

1.

_____   _____   _____

2.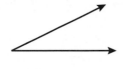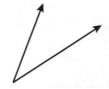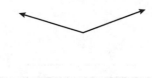

_____   _____   _____

3.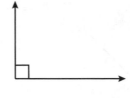

_____   _____   _____

4.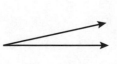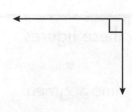

_____   _____   _____

Lesson 11.7 Parallel and Perpendicular Lines

Parallel lines never intersect. They are always the same distance apart.

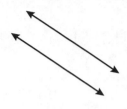

Perpendicular lines cross over each other, or intersect, to form right angles.

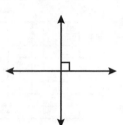

Intersecting lines cross over each other or intersect.

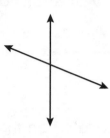

Identify each pair of lines as parallel, perpendicular, or intersecting.

	a	b	c	d

1.

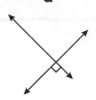

_____ _____ _____ _____

2.

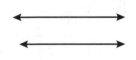

_____ _____ _____ _____

3.

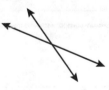   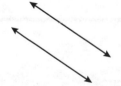   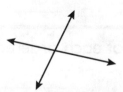

_____ _____ _____ _____

4.

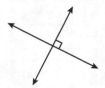   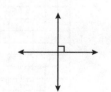

_____ _____ _____ _____

Lesson 11.8 Ordered Pairs on a Coordinate Plane

The x axis runs on a horizontal line.

The y axis runs on a vertical line.

→ x ← x axis

↑ y axis

Points located on the same grid are called **coordinate points**, or **coordinates**.

A point on a grid is located by using an ordered pair. An ordered pair lists an x axis point first and then a y axis point.

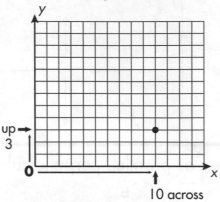

up→ 3

10 across

(10, 3)
 x y

First: Count across ten lines.

Second: From that point, go up three.

Third: Draw a point.

Identify the ordered pair from each grid.

a

1.

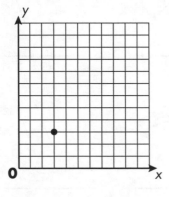

_____

b

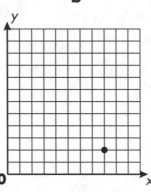

_____

c

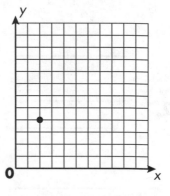

_____

Plot each ordered pair.

2.

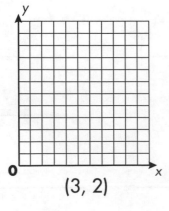

(3, 2)

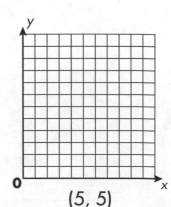

(2, 3)

(5, 5)

Check What You Learned

Geometry

Identify the plane figures.

     a   b   c

1. 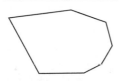 _____ 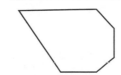 _____ 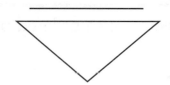 _____

2. _____   _____   _____

Identify the solid figures.

3. _____   _____ 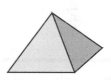 _____

4. 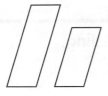 _____ 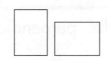 _____ 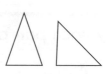 _____

Identify each pair of plane figures as congruent or not congruent.

5. _____   _____   _____

Check What You Learned

Geometry

Identify how each figure has been moved by writing slide, flip, or turn.

a	b	c

6.

_____   _____   _____

Identify each ordered pair.

7. 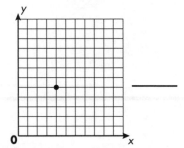 _____   _____   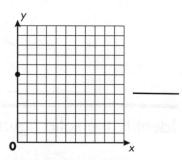 _____

Identify the following geometric figures.

a	b	c	d

8.

_____   _____   _____   _____

Identify each angle as right, acute, or obtuse.

9.

_____   _____   _____   _____

Identify each pair of lines as parallel, perpendicular, or intersecting.

10.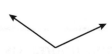

_____   _____   _____   _____

Check What You Know

Preparing for Algebra

Complete the number patterns.

	a	b
1.	2, 3, 5, 2, ☐, ☐, ☐	20, 30, 10, 40, 20, ☐, ☐, ☐
2.	75, 50, 25, 10, 75, ☐, ☐, ☐	1, 3, 5, 1, 3, ☐, ☐, ☐

Determine the number patterns and complete.

3.	5, 10, 15, 20, ☐, ☐, ☐	510, 508, 506, ☐, ☐, ☐
4.	4, 8, 16, 32, ☐, ☐, ☐	78, 87, 99, 114, ☐, 153, ☐

Complete the geometric patterns.

5. ○, ☐, △, ○, ___, ___, ___   ◇, ◇, ⬡, ◇, ○, ○, ◇, ___, ___, ___

6. ▨, ●, △, ▨, ___, ___, ___   •, ↗, ↗, ↗, •, ___, ___, ___

NAME _____

 Check What You Know

Preparing for Algebra

Complete the following.

| | a | b | c |

7. $6 + 5 = 5 + \boxed{}$ $15 + \boxed{} + 16 = 16 + 30 + 15$ $7 + 3 = 2 + \boxed{}$

8. $25 \times 3 = 3 \times \boxed{}$ $2 \times 3 \times 7 = 7 \times 3 \times \boxed{}$ $125 \times 3 = 3 \times \boxed{}$

| | a | b |

9. $17 + (10 + \boxed{}) = (10 + 17) + 6$ $6 \times (5 \times 2) = (6 \times 2) \times \boxed{}$

10. $235 + (10 + 375) = (375 + \boxed{}) + 10$ $14 \times (2 \times 5) = (14 \times 5) \times \boxed{}$

SHOW YOUR WORK

Solve each problem. Write a number sentence to model each word problem.

11. Rosa needs 3 people to carry away the 75 books she has. Each person should carry the same number of books.

How many books should each person carry?

$\boxed{} \underline{} \boxed{} = \boxed{}$

Each person should carry _____ books.

11.

12. Chris's fish collection is growing. He started with 4 fish and now he has 96 fish. How many new fish does he have?

$\boxed{} \underline{} \boxed{} = \boxed{}$

He has _____ new fish.

12.

NAME _____

Lesson 12.1 Repeating Number Patterns

To find the missing number in a sequence, look for repeating numbers and a repeating pattern.

$$3, 4, 7, 3, 3, 4, \boxed{}, 3$$

Each number repeats in a repeating pattern. The pattern starts with 3 and ends with 3. What number is missing in the sequence? 7

So 7 would complete the pattern. $3, 4, 7, 3, 3, 4, \boxed{7}, 3$

Complete the number patterns.

        a   **b**

1. $4, 7, 4, 8, 7, 4, 7, 4, 8, \boxed{}, 4, 7, \boxed{}, 8$

          $300, 200, 1, 300, 200, \boxed{}, \boxed{}, \boxed{}$

2. $78, 45, 23, 14, 78, 45, \boxed{}, 14, \boxed{}$

         $12, 45, 100, 30, 2, 12, 45, \boxed{}, \boxed{}, \boxed{}$

3. $45, 36, 24, 45, 36, \boxed{}, \boxed{}, \boxed{}$

         $100, 10, 200, 20, \boxed{}, \boxed{}, \boxed{}$

4. $75, 5, 36, 6, 75, 5, \boxed{}, \boxed{}$

         $25, 24, 22, 52, 56, 25, 24, \boxed{}, \boxed{}, 56$

5. $470, 590, 230, 470, 590, \boxed{}$

         $15, 13, 15, 13, \boxed{}, \boxed{}, \boxed{}$

6. $250, 240, 750, 230, 250, 240, \boxed{}, 230$

         $780, 960, 52, 11, 780, \boxed{}, 52, \boxed{}$

Lesson 12.2　Growing Number Patterns

Increasing Pattern

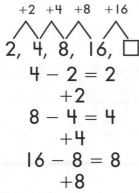

2, 4, 8, 16, □

4 − 2 = 2
+2
8 − 4 = 4
+4
16 − 8 = 8
+8

Think: Each number is added to itself to create the increasing pattern.

16 + 16 = 32

The missing number is 32.

To find a missing number in a growing pattern:
1. Find the difference between numbers that are next to each other.
2. The differences in the number series will show the pattern.
3. Add or subtract to find the missing numbers.

Decreasing Pattern

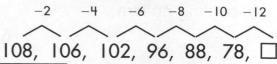

108, 106, 102, 96, 88, 78, □

108 − 106 = 2
−2
106 − 102 = 4
−4
102 − 96 = 6
−6
96 − 88 = 8
−8
88 − 78 = 10
−10

Think: Count by 2s to get the number for the decreasing pattern.

78 − 12 = 66

The missing number is 66.

Complete each pattern.

	a	**b**
1.	11, 15, 20, 26, 33, □ , □	9, 12, 18, 27, □ , 54, □
2.	1, 2, 4, 7, □ , 16, 22	16, 28, 52, 100, 196, □
3.	5, 7, 11, 17, □ , 35, □	158, 156, 152, 146, □ , □ , □
4.	1128, 1096, 1032, 936, □	88, 110, 154, 220, □ , □
5.	460, 450, 430, □ , 360, □	923, 915, 904, 890, □ , □
6.	180, 176, 168, 156, 140, □	64, 74, 86, 100, □
7.	□ , □ , 65, 80, 100, 125	□ , □ , 54, 96, 152, 222

Lesson 12.3   Geometric Patterns

What are the next 2 objects
in this pattern?

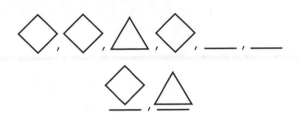

Cross out the object that is not in the
correct sequence.

What should be the correct object?

The object should be a hexagon.

Draw the next 2 objects in each pattern.

a	**b**

1.    ▽,▷,△,◁,___,___

2.    

3.    

Find the object that is out of sequence. Cross it out. Draw the correct object on the blank line.

4.    

5.    

Lesson 12.4   Number Sentences

$7 + 5 \quad 6 + 6$	$7 \times 4 \quad 14 \times 2$	$153 \times 11 \quad 11 \times 153$	$167 + 2 \quad 2 + 167$
$12 \;=\; 12$	$28 \;=\; 28$	$1683 \;=\; 1683$	$169 \;=\; 169$
$7 + 5 = 6 + 6$	$7 \times 4 = 14 \times 2$	$153 \times 11 = 11 \times 153$	$167 + 2 = 2 + 167$

Fill in the missing number. Show your work.

	a	**b**	**c**
1.	$8 + 2 = 4 + \boxed{}$ 6	$25 \times 3 = \boxed{} \times 25$ 3	$764 + 2 = 2 + \boxed{}$ 764
2.	$153 + 62 = 62 + \boxed{}$	$17 \times 2 = 2 \times \boxed{}$	$12 \times 13 = 4 \times \boxed{}$
3.	$1250 + 23 = 23 + \boxed{}$	$75 \times 5 = 15 \times \boxed{}$	$12 + 8 = \boxed{} + 15$
4.	$33 + 33 = 11 \times \boxed{}$	$230 \times 4 = \boxed{} \times 230$	$513 + 32 = \boxed{} + 513$
5.	$60 + 52 = 100 + \boxed{}$	$4 \times 8 = 16 \times \boxed{}$	$25 \times 4 = 2 \times \boxed{}$

Lesson 12.5 Number Sentences

Multiply numbers in parentheses first.

$$2 \times (3 \times 15) = (2 \times 3) \times 15$$
$$2 \times 45 = 6 \times 15$$
$$2 \times (3 \times 15) = (2 \times 3) \times 15$$

Add numbers in parentheses first.

$$(15 + 2) + 6 = 15 + (2 + 6)$$
$$17 + 6 = 15 + 8$$
$$23 = 23$$
$$(15 + 2) + 6 = 15 + (2 + 6)$$

Find the missing number. Show your work.

	a	**b**

1. $(7 \times 5) \times 2 = (5 \times \boxed{}) \times 7$ $\qquad$ $(135 + 30) + 17 = (17 + 30) + \boxed{}$

$\underline{\quad 2 \quad}$ $\qquad\qquad\qquad\qquad$ $\underline{\quad 135 \quad}$

2. $(190 + 70) + 30 = (30 + 70) + \boxed{}$ $\qquad$ $(77 \times 5) \times 6 = (77 \times 6) \times \boxed{}$

$\underline{\qquad\qquad}$ $\qquad\qquad\qquad\qquad$ $\underline{\qquad\qquad}$

3. $(25 + 23) + 17 = (17 + 23) + \boxed{}$ $\qquad$ $(25 \times 10) \times 2 = (10 \times 2) \times \boxed{}$

$\underline{\qquad\qquad}$ $\qquad\qquad\qquad\qquad$ $\underline{\qquad\qquad}$

4. $(1245 + 132) + 50 = (132 + 50) + \boxed{}$ $\qquad$ $(130 \times 3) \times 5 = (3 \times 5) \times \boxed{}$

$\underline{\qquad\qquad}$ $\qquad\qquad\qquad\qquad$ $\underline{\qquad\qquad}$

5. $(\boxed{} + 35) + 70 = (70 + 20) + 35$ $\qquad$ $(93 \times \boxed{}) \times 4 = (4 \times 15) \times 93$

$\underline{\qquad\qquad}$ $\qquad\qquad\qquad\qquad$ $\underline{\qquad\qquad}$

6. $(25 + 17) + 3 = (17 + 3) + \boxed{}$ $\qquad$ $175 + (32 + 14) = (175 + 14) + \boxed{}$

$\underline{\qquad\qquad}$ $\qquad\qquad\qquad\qquad$ $\underline{\qquad\qquad}$

Lesson 12.5 Problem Solving

Write a number sentence below each problem.
Then, solve each problem.

1. Zeb has to buy 7 washers for each bolt he puts into his deck. If he uses 63 bolts, how many washers does he need?

   $$\boxed{}\ \underline{}\ \boxed{} = \boxed{}$$

   $$63 \times 7 = 441$$

   Zeb will need ____441____ washers.

   1.

2. For one week, the toy store gave away 2 bottles of bubbles with every order. There were 182 orders. How many bottles of bubbles were given away?

   $$\boxed{}\ \underline{}\ \boxed{} = \boxed{}$$

   The store gave away _____ bottles.

   2.

3. Manny is stocking shelves with bags of dry noodles. If there are 58 bags of noodles and 29 bags fit on a shelf, how many shelves will he use?

   $$\boxed{}\ \underline{}\ \boxed{} = \boxed{}$$

   Manny will use _____ shelves.

   3.

4. The Smith family needs to buy sunglasses for their trip. There are 5 members in the family, and the glasses cost $12.32 per pair. How much will it cost to buy everyone a pair?

   $$\boxed{}\ \underline{}\ \boxed{} = \boxed{}$$

   The cost for the sunglasses will be _____.

   4.

5. Linda is collecting money to buy the teacher a gift. If she collects $17.50 on Monday, $18.50 on Tuesday, and $12.50 on Wednesday, how much will she collect for all 3 days?

   $$\boxed{}\ \underline{}\ \boxed{}\ \underline{}\ \boxed{} = \boxed{}$$

   Linda will collect _____.

   5.

Check What You Learned

Preparing for Algebra

Complete the number patterns.

        a   **b**

1.   25, 24, 23, 25, ☐ , ☐   256, 257, 256, 258, ☐ , ☐

2.   66, 55, 44, ☐ , ☐   570, 551, 531, 510, ☐ , 465, ☐ , ☐

3.   14, 28, 44, 62, ☐ , ☐   ☐ , 26, ☐ , 42, 53, 66, 81

Draw the objects that complete the pattern.

4.   ⊘, ⊘, ⊘, ⊘, __, __   ☐, ☐, ◺, ◺, ☐, __, __

5.   ⊕, ◔, ◔, ⊞, ◧, ◧, ⊕, ◔, __, __, __

Check What You Learned

Preparing for Algebra

Complete the number sentences.

	a	**b**
6.	$(7 \times 3) \times 5 = (5 \times \square) \times 7$	$516 + (432 + 75) = (516 + 432) + \square$
7.	$12 + 3 = 10 + \square$	$9 \times 4 = 6 \times \square$
8.	$7 \times 6 = \square \times 7$	$25 \times 4 = 5 \times \square$

SHOW YOUR WORK

Write a number sentence below each problem. Then, solve each problem.

9. Claudia wants to ride the bus downtown. A round-trip costs $2.45. Claudia has $1.13 in her purse. How much more money does she need?

$\square \underline{} \square = \square$

Claudia needs _____ more to ride the bus.

9.

10. In the AuraStars football game, 15 points were scored in the first quarter and 25 points were scored in the second quarter. Only 2 points were scored in the rest of the game. How many points were scored in the game?

$\square \underline{} \square \underline{} \square = \square$

The teams scored _____ points in the game.

10.

Final Test Chapters 1–12

Add.

	a	**b**	**c**	**d**	**e**
1.	21 +15	1932 + 32	718 + 72	247 + 38	1005 + 49
2.	2498 +1832	787 +193	6918 +5832	957 + 98	2950 + 709
3.	25765 + 5403	7864 +3258	20048 7212 + 500	18970 + 2718	50908 7312 + 8903

Subtract.

	a	**b**	**c**	**d**	**e**
4.	98 − 7	87 − 8	54 − 6	48 − 9	60 − 7
5.	705 −178	6005 − 736	7132 −5600	9568 −7432	900 −445
6.	461 − 32	1353 − 72	777 − 23	2525 − 518	905 − 87

Spectrum Math
Grade 4

Final Test
Chapters 1–12

CHAPTERS 1–12 FINAL TEST

161

Final Test Chapters 1–12

Multiply.

	a	b	c	d	e
7.	78 × 9	56 × 8	97 × 9	48 × 8	25 × 9
8.	98 × 98	78 × 15	48 × 36	77 × 54	83 × 27
9.	702 × 36	389 × 18	215 × 48	247 × 32	509 × 78
10.	7035 × 42	2003 × 42	3972 × 68	5931 × 24	2450 × 50

Divide.

11. $3\overline{)45}$	$9\overline{)72}$	$4\overline{)66}$	$5\overline{)94}$	$5\overline{)85}$
12. $6\overline{)493}$	$3\overline{)873}$	$7\overline{)875}$	$5\overline{)987}$	$8\overline{)800}$
13. $7\overline{)2598}$	$2\overline{)5282}$	$6\overline{)5631}$	$4\overline{)9637}$	$5\overline{)2515}$
14. $6\overline{)9832}$	$8\overline{)5000}$	$5\overline{)7004}$	$7\overline{)5111}$	$8\overline{)9840}$

Final Test Chapters 1–12

Determine the place value of the underlined digit in each number.

15. 15.7̲5 _____   1̲2,372 _____

16. 72.056̲ _____   103,7̲28 _____

Round each the number to the place of the underlined number.

17. 103,4̲67 _____   1̲,785,302 _____

18. 23̲,456 _____   57̲5 _____

Write >, <, or = to compare the following.

19. 14.05 ◯ 14.95   12,700 ◯ 12,703   164,000 ◯ 146,000

20. 17.05 ◯ 17.05   0.008 ◯ 0.010   0.010 ◯ 0.100

Estimate each sum or difference.

	a	b	c	d	e
21.	5205 −3800	157321 + 58538	3852 + 28	72550 − 8549	4983 +3872

Add or subtract.

	a	b	c	d
22.	$\frac{5}{6} + \frac{1}{6} =$ _____	$\frac{7}{12} + \frac{3}{12} =$ _____	$\frac{6}{8} - \frac{4}{8} =$ _____	$\frac{11}{12} - \frac{7}{12} =$ _____

Find an equivalent fraction.

23. $\frac{8}{32} = \frac{}{4}$ $\frac{1}{10} = \frac{}{40}$ $\frac{4}{100} = \frac{1}{}$ $\frac{7}{8} = \frac{49}{}$

Spectrum Math
Grade 4

Final Test
Chapters 1–12
163

CHAPTERS 1–12 FINAL TEST

Final Test Chapters 1–12

Add or subtract.

	a	b	c	d
24.	$15.32 + 4.32	0.159 −0.108	75¢ −25¢	4.012 +3.710

Complete the following.

	a	b	c
25.	36 in. = _____ yd.	7 cm = _____ mm	5 T. = _____ lb.
26.	12 c. = _____ pt.	72 kg = _____ g	132 ft. = _____ yd.
27.	20 m = _____ mm	14 km = _____ m	22 L = _____ mL

Find the perimeter of each shape.

28.

5 ft. 3 ft. 3 ft. ____ ft.

10 in. 10 in. 10 in. 10 in. ____ in.

15 m 7 m 7 m 15 m ____ m

Find the area of each rectangle.

29.

30 ft. 5 ft. ____ sq. ft.

22 cm 8 cm ____ sq. cm

10 in. 30 in. ____ sq. in.

82 mm 25 mm ____ sq. mm

Use graph to answer each question.

30. What item was sold the most? _____

How many cookies were sold? _____

Items Sold at School Bake Sale

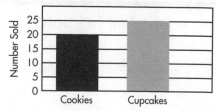

CHAPTERS 1–12 FINAL TEST

Final Test Chapters 1–12

Use the spinner to find probability.

31. What is the probability of spinning a **2**? _____

What is the probability of spinning a **1**? _____

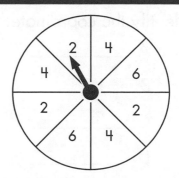

Identify the figures below.

      a   **b**   **c**   **d**   **e**

32.

_____   _____   _____   _____   _____

33.

_____   _____   _____   _____   _____

Identify each pair of lines as parallel, perpendicular, or intersecting.

      a   **b**   **c**

34.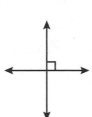

_____   _____   _____

Write the next number in the sequence.

      a   **b**

35. 45, 48, 51, ☐   52, 57, 64, 73, 84, ☐ , ☐

36. 1245, 1195, 1145, ☐   ☐ , 25, ☐ , 75, 100, ☐ , 150, 175

Spectrum Math
Grade 4

Final Test
Chapters 1–12
165

CHAPTERS 1-12 FINAL TEST

Final Test Chapters 1–12

Identify the coordinates on the grid.

37. A _____

B _____

C _____

D _____

E _____

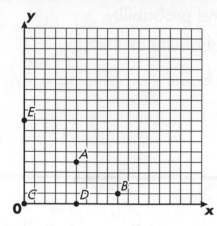

Complete the number sentences.

	a		**b**

38. $7 \times 15 = 5 \times \boxed{}$ $(22 \times 8) \times 3 = (8 \times 3) \times \boxed{}$

39. $(300 \times 2) \times 5 = (300 \times 2) \times \boxed{}$ $(5 + 6) + 10 = (\boxed{} + 6) + 5$

40. $(75 + 30) + 25 = (75 + 25) + \boxed{}$ $(225 + 3) + 1 = (\boxed{} + 1) + 225$

SHOW YOUR WORK

Write each number sentence. Then, solve each problem.

41. The track team ran 10 miles on Saturday. There are 1,760 yards in a mile. How many yards did the track team run?

The track team ran _____ yards.

41.

42. A certain type of blue snake can grow to 28 feet. There are 3 of these snakes in the local zoo. How many feet of blue snakes will the zoo have when these 3 are fully grown?

The zoo will have _____ feet of blue snakes.

42.

Scoring Record for Posttests, Mid-Test, and Final Test

Chapter Posttest	Your Score	Performance			
		Excellent	Very Good	Fair	Needs Improvement
1	____of 65	61–65	53–60	40–52	39 or fewer
2	____of 62	59–62	51–58	38–50	37 or fewer
3	____of 45	43–45	37–42	28–36	27 or fewer
4	____of 48	46–48	39–45	30–38	29 or fewer
5	____of 56	53–56	46–52	35–45	34 or fewer
6	____of 31	30–31	26–29	20–25	19 or fewer
7	____of 40	38–40	33–37	25–32	24 or fewer
8	____of 23	22–23	19–21	15–18	14 or fewer
9	____of 34	33–34	28–32	21–27	20 or fewer
10	____of 13	13	11–12	9–10	8 or fewer
11	____of 33	32–33	27–31	21–26	20 or fewer
12	____of 28	27–28	23–26	18–22	17 or fewer
Mid-Test	____of 182	170–182	147–169	110–146	109 or fewer
Final Test	____of 156	146–156	126–145	95–125	94 or fewer

Record your test score in the Your Score column. See where your score falls in the Performance columns. Your score is based on the total number of required responses. If your score is fair or needs improvement, review the chapter material.

Grade 4 Answers

Chapter 1

Pretest, page 1

	a	b	c	d	e	f
1.	38	38	99	25	49	87
2.	67	59	94	98	55	89
3.	83	97	57	98	69	79
4.	19	48	78	89	96	77
5.	41	52	52	64	62	13
6.	22	11	21	52	21	32
7.	10	45	12	71	14	11
8.	31	11	10	33	62	21

Pretest, page 2

9. 56 **10.** 36 **11.** 21 **12.** 32 **13.** 21 **14.** 11

Lesson 1.1, page 3

	a	b	c	d	e	f
1.	19	40	39	99	69	97
2.	90	9	19	99	77	80
3.	29	50	99	99	69	90
4.	43	60	99	58	29	70
5.	45	42	49	80	97	79
6.	68	73	39	7	19	77
7.	35	15	87	91	49	62

Lesson 1.2, page 4

	a	b	c	d	e	f
1.	21	23	61	5	70	61
2.	64	21	12	10	31	10
3.	10	90	20	32	17	1
4.	13	11	8	13	7	2
5.	31	71	32	61	71	1
6.	44	10	4	14	11	52
7.	12	51	23	15	22	22

Lesson 1.3, page 5

	a	b	c	d	e	f	g	h
1.	12	11	15	16	17	18	17	14
2.	18	10	13	16	19	20	17	13
3.	20	16	13	16	21	18	16	21
4.	16	19	22	18	14	25	19	21
5.	20	19	25	14	17	17	26	18
6.	19	22	18	19	22	21	20	16

Lesson 1.4, page 6

	a	b	c	d	e	f
1.	51	47	80	31	80	35
2.	91	64	74	81	34	70
3.	91	78	50	90	84	91
4.	63	62	81	70	54	90
5.	90	57	84	91	37	80
6.	68	56	38	85	33	81
7.	82	82	72	96	38	60

Lesson 1.5, page 7

	a	b	c	d	e	f
1.	102	163	194	245	167	139
2.	208	138	220	222	170	276
3.	115	260	144	136	198	105
4.	231	207	230	243	214	166
5.	310	124	242	222	198	227
6.	204	204	222	203	123	231

Lesson 1.6, page 8

	a	b	c	d	e	f
1.	137	115	119	105	116	118
2.	109	118	105	108	119	134
3.	112	146	119	115	143	134
4.	115	109	115	115	107	116
5.	132	119	115	119	126	119
6.	109	136	127	138	133	136
7.	119	128	136	109	125	118

Lesson 1.6, page 9

	a	b	c	d	e	f
1.	79	83	89	69	89	89
2.	82	86	88	86	83	87
3.	77	78	89	89	78	86
4.	34	77	67	79	69	73
5.	89	78	79	86	86	58
6.	88	86	58	79	87	46
7.	69	48	77	49	69	78

Lesson 1.7, page 10

	a	b	c	d	e	f
1.	79	82	62	99	43	90
2.	75	92	94	71	55	71
3.	90	61	90	142	193	274
4.	213	161	175	141	182	166

Lesson 1.8, page 11

	a	b	c	d	e	f
1.	43	4	19	57	47	25
2.	21	41	18	17	19	39
3.	127	94	97	38	79	85
4.	88	99	119	69	98	86

Lesson 1.9, page 12

1. 86 **2.** 173 **3.** 207 **4.** 335 **5.** 164

Posttest, page 13

	a	b	c	d	e	f
1.	70	78	52	101	299	100
2.	31	55	306	246	211	204
3.	34	295	165	176	121	82
4.	104	480	64	100	136	87
5.	92	180	135	181	200	108
6.	213	89	23	44	18	28

7.	73	69	189	39	145	11
8.	19	89	19	110	115	58
9.	99	40	25	99	75	63
10.	149	37	78	19	109	19

Posttest, page 14

11. 100 **12.** 112 **13.** 82 **14.** 200 **15.** 295

Chapter 2

Pretest, page 15

1a. 3,000 + 200 + 40 + 5   **1b.** 900 + 70 + 3
1c. 50 + 1
2a. 6,000 + 600 + 70 + 5
2b. 800,000 + 40,000 + 5,000 + 400 + 50
2c. 700 + 90

	a	b
3.	4	3
4.	2	5
5.	9	9

6a. 4,312 > 4,213 **6b.** 95 > 58 **6c.** 408 < 480
7a. 52,650 > 52,560 **7b.** 610 < 672 **7c.** 72 > 62
8a. 52,173 < 520,173 **8b.** 4,675,321 < 4,751,670
8c. 25 < 52
9a. 158,325 = 158,325 **9b.** 652 > 256
9c. 8,910,003 = 8,910,003

Pretest, page 16

	a	b	c
10.	8,000	900	600,000
11.	10,000,000	80	1,700
12.	80,000	930	682,000

	a	b	c	d
13.	90,000	9	900,000	90
14.	9,000,000	9,000	9,000	90,000
15.	900	9	90,000	9,000,000

Lesson 2.1, page 17

1a. 50 + 4 **1b.** 600 + 8
1c. 30 + 2 **1d.** 400 + 20 + 1
2a. 400 + 30 **2b.** 500 + 40 + 9
2c. 70 + 5 **2d.** 600 + 90 + 9
3a. 100 + 30 + 2 **3b.** 700 + 20 + 1
3c. 30 + 9 **3d.** 80 + 7
4a. 900 + 10 + 1 **4b.** 500 + 10 + 3
4c. 100 + 90 **4d.** 70

	a	b	c	d
5.	70	900	6	4
6.	700	60	0	900

	a	b
7.	0; hundreds	4; hundreds
8.	7; ones	4; tens

Lesson 2.2, page 18

1a. 3,000 + 400 + 60 + 5
1b. 20,000 + 5,000 + 600 + 30 + 9
1c. 40,000 + 3,000 + 600 + 40 + 5
2a. 20,000 + 4,000
2b. 60,000 + 9,000 + 3
2c. 90,000 + 300 + 20 + 7
3a. 50,000 + 2,000 + 300 + 4
3b. 60,000 + 5,000 + 700 + 90 + 2
3c. 4,000 + 9

	a	b
4.	7; ten thousands	3; hundreds
5.	9; thousands	5; hundreds
6.	7; ten thousands	1; ones

	a	b	c
7.	50,000	7,000	700
8.	90	60,000	3,000

Lesson 2.3, page 19

	a	b
1.	5; ten thousands	2; hundred thousands
2.	6; hundreds	5; hundred thousands
3.	5	9
4.	9	0
5.	6	9

6a. 600,000 + 50,000 + 3,000 + 400 + 10
6b. 70,000 + 6,000 + 900 + 80 + 2
7a. 60,000 + 2,000 + 500 + 10 + 2
7b. 100,000 + 3,000 + 200 + 50 + 4
8a. 100,000 + 90,000 + 9,000 + 400 + 80 + 2
8b. 30,000 + 2,000 + 400 + 50 + 1

Lesson 2.4, page 20

	a	b	c	d
1.	5,000,000	50,000	60	5
2.	800,000	7,000	1,000,000	4,000

3a. 2,000,000 + 500,000 + 50 + 5
3b. 500,000 + 10,000 + 3,000 + 400 + 60 + 8
4a. 500,000 + 90,000 + 8,000 + 700 + 20 + 1
4b. 9,000,000 + 300,000 + 40,000 + 2,000 +
700 + 50 + 1
5a. 300,000 + 70,000 + 1,000 + 80 + 8
5b. 80,000 + 1,000 + 200 + 3
6a. 5; hundred thousands **6b.** 3; millions
7a. 6; ten thousands **7b.** 9; millions
8a. 8; hundred thousands **8b.** 4; millions

Lesson 2.5, page 21

1a. 6,420 **1b.** 5,880 **1c.** 45,290
1d. 980 **1e.** 13,940 **1f.** 840
2a. 9,860 **2b.** 26,920 **2c.** 980
2d. 95,650 **2e.** 8,670 **2f.** 29,980

Grade 4 Answers

3a. 325,800 **3b.** 49,800 **3c.** 123,700
3d. 24,600 **3e.** 199,800 **3f.** 79,300
4a. 798,800 **4b.** 58,300 **4c.** 9,900
4d. 8,400 **4e.** 10,100 **4f.** 1,987,700
5a. 568,000 **5b.** 94,000 **5c.** 4,000
5d. 12,000 **5e.** 747,000 **5f.** 9,000
6a. 987,000 **6b.** 346,000 **6c.** 98,000
6d. 9,000 **6e.** 75,000 **6f.** 187,000

Lesson 2.5, page 22
1a. 730,000 **1b.** 1,460,000 **1c.** 740,000
1d. 5,550,000 **1e.** 50,000
2a. 180,000 **2b.** 7,740,000 **2c.** 30,000
2d. 480,000 **2e.** 5,640,000
3a. 4,800,000 **3b.** 400,000 **3c.** 9,300,000
3d. 8,000,000 **3e.** 500,000
4a. 8,700,000 **4b.** 1,100,000 **4c.** 400,000
4d. 9,700,000 **4e.** 600,000
5a. 7,000,000 **5b.** 7,000,000 **5c.** 2,000,000
5d. 4,000,000 **5e.** 8,000,000
6a. 2,000,000 **6b.** 4,000,000 **6c.** 7,000,000
6d. 6,000,000 **6e.** 8,000,000

Lesson 2.6, page 23
1a. 105 < 120 **1b.** 52 > 35 **1c.** 10,362 < 10,562
2a. 5,002 > 2,113 **2b.** 713 < 731
2c. 12,317 > 11,713
3a. 115,000 > 105,000 **3b.** 23 < 32;
3c. 142 = 142
4a. 310 > 290 **4b.** 715 < 725
4c. 1,132,700 > 1,032,700
5a. 616 > 106 **5b.** 119,000 < 120,000
5c. 48,112 < 48,212
6a. 823 > 821 **6b.** 2,003,461 < 2,004,461
6c. 7,903 < 9,309
7a. 30 > 25 **7b.** 47,999 > 45,999
7c. 19,900 > 19,090
8a. 111 = 111 **8b.** 386,712 > 386,711
8c. 615 > 614

Lesson 2.6, page 24
1a. 3,647 < 36,647 **1b.** 4,678 < 4,768
1c. 68,035 > 68,025
2a. 4,102,364 < 4,201,364 **2b.** 56,703 > 56,702
2c. 125,125 < 125,150
3a. 90,368 < 90,369 **3b.** 5,654,308 > 5,546,309
3c. 65,003 < 65,013
4a. 4,567,801 > 456,780 **4b.** 7,621 > 7,261
4c. 769,348 > 759,348
5a. 506,708 < 506,807 **5b.** 1,365,333 = 1,365,333
5c. 9,982 > 9,928
6a. 224,364 < 234,364 **6b.** 32,506 > 23,605

6c. 7,850 = 7,850
7a. 3,204,506 < 3,204,606 **7b.** 9,851 > 9,850
7c. 2,000,567 < 2,001,567
8a. 430,632 < 480,362 **8b.** 49,984 = 49,984
8c. 5,640,002 > 5,639,992
9a. 172,302 < 173,302 **9b.** 212,304 = 212,304
9c. 6,886 < 6,896

Posttest, page 25
1a. 1,000,000 + 900,000 + 60,000 + 5,000 + 10 + 2
1b. 600,000 + 90,000 + 3,000 + 100 + 40 + 5
2a. 100,000 + 3,000 + 400 + 50 + 8
2b. 20,000 + 3,000 + 900 + 70 + 2
3a. 400,000 + 70,000 + 1,000 + 400 + 40
3b. 10,000 + 8,000 + 300 + 20 + 1
4a. 90,000 + 8,000 + 400 + 80 + 5
4b. 300,000 + 10,000 + 3,000 + 80 + 2

	a	b	c	d
5.	5,000	0	100	10
6.	40,000	800,000	80	8,000
7.	3,000,000	500,000	60	3

Posttest, page 26
8a. 2,400,000 **8b.** 760,000 **8c.** 90,000
8d. 2,390,000 **8e.** 630,000
9a. 310,000 **9b.** 8,940,000 **9c.** 430,000
9d. 50,000 **9e.** 2,010,000
10a. 3,000,000 **10b.** 800,000 **10c.** 3,100,000
10d. 900,000 **10e.** 400,000
11a. 500,000 **11b.** 7,700,000 **11c.** 200,000
11d. 6,500,000 **11e.** 500,000
12a. 2,000,000 **12b.** 9,000,000 **12c.** 7,000,000
12d. 5,000,000 **12e.** 7,000,000
13a. 2,000,000 **13b.** 7,000,000 **13c.** 9,000,000
13d. 3,000,000 **13e.** 6,000,000
14a. 24,124 < 24,224 **14b.** 1,975,212 < 1,985,212
14c. 56,410 > 54,408
15a. 509,712 < 590,172
15b. 2,341,782 = 2,341,782
15c. 976,152 > 967,932
16a. 6,918 > 6,818 **16b.** 49,917 > 49,907
16c. 3,425,556 < 3,524,565
17a. 8,724,100 > 5,724,101
17b. 3,002,019 < 3,002,109 **17c.** 2,418 = 2,418

Chapter 3

Pretest, page 27

	a	b	c	d	e
1.	779	1971	927	3867	6929
2.	5720	310	3588	1248	1877

Grade 4 Answers

3.	680	5,437	7,495	9,899	1,980
4.	4,790	3,998	6,737	1,034	6,000
5.	2,503	542	6,408	111	5,905
6.	8,122	1,901	911	6,102	3,967
7.	2,617	2,281	1,163	1,318	22,011
8.	797	5241	320	69,216	9,393

Pretest, page 28

9. 3,994 10. 25,994 11. 1,398 12. 245
13. 448

Lesson 3.1, page 29

	a	b	c	d	e	f
1.	909	750	589	259	788	993
2.	561	408	720	780	598	1,155
3.	983	396	672	810	757	900
4.	980	431	858	1,270	712	309
5.	889	666	543	387	1,300	950
6.	1,014	457	940	584	857	263
7.	1,193	918	1,010	397	1,099	357

Lesson 3.2, page 30

	a	b	c	d	e	f
1.	911	609	1,133	231	4,796	399
2.	4,498	311	290	3,267	103	1,964
3.	1102	190	6,100	524	101	1,069
4.	7,812	281	910	756	151	1,589
5.	108	2,778	3,482	625	4,444	2,692
6.	223	3,747	5,700	1,251	2613	5,086

Lesson 3.3, page 31

	a	b	c	d	e
1.	2,897	5,028	4,210	11,042	8,712
2.	5,499	9,229	9,992	4,330	9,006
3.	6,651	4,622	3,748	3,776	4,145
4.	3,771	5,410	4,028	9,095	7,990
5.	5,115	3,791	5,908	9,595	7,760
6.	10,100	7,983	7,090	2,784	9,919
7.	14,702	3,182	8,134	4,881	6,989

Lesson 3.4, page 32

1. 5,949 2. 7,077 3. 361 4. 131 5. 920
6. 3,158

Lesson 3.5, page 33

	a	b	c	d	e
1.	19,115	69,600	33,998	11,123	32,422
2.	65,111	12,990	89,341	13,902	78,921
3.	17	55,198	9,097	8,111	33,690
4.	19,002	34,901	78,064	14,009	10,829
5.	32,899	30,993	11,186	14,219	2,101
6.	4,716	9170	15,000	7,653	7,842
7.	52,108	78,999	11,090	27,680	12,576

Lesson 3.6, page 34

	a	b	c	d	e
1.	730	910	1,068	707	2,563
2.	13,727	840	9,974	1,252	2,312
3.	3,872	18,280	12,189	16,563	1,966
4.	6,762	17,920	4,594	13,675	8,201
5.	7,199	12,820	9,053	16,661	11,930

Lesson 3.7, page 35

	a	b	c	d	e
1.	11,557	24,275	9,099	102,380	3,432
2.	29,850	12,598	22,881	10,018	16,516
3.	8,339	48,390	6,889	50,341	91,001
4.	12,065	11,062	78,186	14,807	40,305
5.	3,860	38,900	13,810	65,237	11,099
6.	17,509	8,217	51,510	4,039	30,583

Lesson 3.8, page 36

1. 8,517 2. 13,300 3. 66,640 4. 4,724
5. 40,851

Lesson 3.9, page 37

	a	b	c	d	e
1.	44,113	76,892	68,111	73,107	12,000
2.	2,727	20,038	99,002	4,559	43,663
3.	57,564	47,408	78,012	46,619	8,973
4.	658	3,476	1,730	1,783	9,041
5.	3,556	6,201	1,085	17,191	786
6.	71,359	1,9788	1,765	9,791	2,190
7.	8,421	1,680	49,106	2,096	7,324
8.	57,829	10,038	14,011	1,818	6,884

Lesson 3.10, page 38

	a	b	c	d	e
1.	7,263	2,470	8,675	15,865	3,507
2.	1,793	19,330	111,175	10,086	208
3.	3,988	42,050	38,966	101	884
4.	6,781	49,059	1,009	250	679
5.	5,163	57,806	791	20,470	2,567
6.	639	25,829	11,819	11,590	7,700
7.	2,075	42,601	4,731	10,389	83,546
8.	10,235	18,354	6,566	7,725	13,906

Lesson 3.11, page 39

	a	b	c	d	e
1.	61,000	14,000	1,800	80,000	40,000
2.	13,000	40,000	69,000	1,500	6,200
3.	7,000	110,000	5,000	80,000	59,000
4.	20,000	6,400	1,000	8,000	40,000
5.	0	3,600	48,000	1,000	20,000
6.	1,300	25,600	13,400	60,000	100

Lesson 3.11, page 40

1. 110,000 2. 3,000 3. 14,000 4. 4,700
5. 4,000 6. 6,000

Grade 4 Answers

Posttest, page 41

	a	b	c	d	e
1.	99,013	62,882	1,094	2,600	8,222
2.	26,348	51,609	2,943	13,345	60,012
3.	991	10,050	4,232	111,867	19,991
4.	60,835	1,059	4,024	6,899	28,606
5.	57,818	24,023	659	9,009	18,909
6.	576	337	252	42,753	21,431
7.	56,000	6,000	88,000	8,100	80,000
8.	4500	10,000	79,000	0	6,000

Posttest, page 42

9. 1,028   10. 1,470   11. 3,185   12. 700

13. 11,800

Chapter 4

Pretest, page 43

	a	b	c	d	e	f
1.	56	75	3,926	255	90	144
2.	14,805	81	4,732	1,056	2,821	744
3.	24,200	1,659	2,200	32	2,691	392
4.	17,250	100	1,588	18,75	121	2,916
5.	41,584	1,936	42	4,62	5,694	12,832
6.	18,312	2,310	64	4,578	29,046	15,000
7.	3,060	4,352	25,839	28,512	535	247
8.	7,416	3,740	5,340	360	4,366	45,000

Pretest, page 44

9. 250   10. 198   11. 8,000   12. 2,145   13. 50

Lesson 4.1, page 45

	a	b	c	d	e	f	g	h
1.	9	56	18	35	36	36	7	0
2.	81	12	15	16	49	27	4	9
3.	40	24	16	63	32	21	25	72
4.	1	45	48	42	54	56	21	28
5.	18	0	36	30	14	9	27	48
6.	20	8	10	64	18	42	72	0

Lesson 4.2, page 46

	a	b	c	d	e	f
1.	46	71	48	66	70	48
2.	88	86	90	88	36	28
3.	99	75	66	90	40	84
4.	77	20	0	39	60	62
5.	20	82	26	80	60	55
6.	30	77	25	0	66	10
7.	0	50	93	36	80	70

Lesson 4.3, page 47

	a	b	c	d	e	f
1.	292	50	108	260	92	210
2.	38	52	204	270	376	132
3.	288	384	156	136	85	110
4.	198	225	330	171	342	222
5.	165	512	415	343	450	516
6.	360	51	432	225	540	480
7.	279	308	246	288	280	158

Lesson 4.4, page 48

1. 432   2. 141   3. 368   4. 188   5. 168   6. 115

Lesson 4.5, page 49

	a	b	c	d	e	f
1.	354	1,220	1,120	456	1,400	685
2.	981	474	1,410	1,278	1,740	1,161
3.	1,675	1,330	3,368	1,809	861	972
4.	2,025	944	1,206	2,988	4,900	796
5.	1,956	568	5,632	1,351	738	1,064
6.	4,224	2,253	1,400	1,110	1,818	5,110

Lesson 4.6, page 50

	a	b	c	d	e	f
1.	726	495	800	713	156	930
2.	861	640	400	651	900	140
3.	968	280	480	900	169	330
4.	770	132	810	288	880	961

Lesson 4.7, page 51

	a	b	c	d	e	f
1.	418	1,312	1,296	675	960	1,694
2.	1,512	2,496	700	2,310	957	6,300
3.	1,311	324	2,079	1,105	1,936	1,800
4.	851	3,458	1,892	221	1,496	2,090

Lesson 4.8, page 52

	a	b	c	d	e	f
1.	9,450	22,134	6,027	16,940	6,270	13,821
2.	4,480	4508	61,916	26,016	24,160	6,750
3.	47,771	37,800	14,256	29,754	59,711	31,836
4.	9,125	21,886	14,784	9,708	44,895	38,014

Lesson 4.9, page 53

	a	b	c	d	e	f
1.	729	92	441	66	702	282
2.	720	180	156	88	365	696
3.	1,395	609	4,120	450	6,419	4,266
4.	1,032	1,236	990	4,218	8,100	5,312
5.	2,736	1,127	544	2,700	588	2,176
6.	486	1,760	3,311	1,560	323	1,296

Lesson 4.10, page 54

1. 96   2. 396   3. 750   4. 825   5. 120   6. 80

Posttest, page 55

1a. 288   1b. 192   1c. 678   1d. 272

1e. 1,350   1f. 666   1g. 186

2a. 484   2b. 512   2c. 217   2d. 6,300

Grade 4 Answers

2e. 63 **2f.** 4844 **2g.** 720
3a. 56 **3b.** 728 **3c.** 66 **3d.** 4347
3e. 5400 **3f.** 316 **3g.** 4501
4a. 1486 **4b.** 4390 **4c.** 2691 **4d.** 5658
4e. 48 **4f.** 1800 **4g.** 22200
5a. 1722 **5b.** 3732 **5c.** 1296 **5d.** 132
5e. 21294 **5f.** 2565 **5g.** 6001
6a. 7272 **6b.** 24366 **6c.** 6666 **6d.** 2548
6e. 1204 **6f.** 6110 **6g.** 22165

Posttest, page 56

7. 460 **8.** 252 **9.** 14880 **10.** 750 **11.** 805
12. 180

Chapter 5

Pretest, page 57

	a	b	c	d	e
1.	5	7	3	9	3
2.	6	6	9	8	5
3.	9	4	8	5	9
4.	2	7	4	3	6
5.	3	7	6	4	7
6.	6	8	4	8	3
7.	9	8	5	1	0
8.	7	4	9	7	6
9.	9	9	7	1	4
10.	5	7	8	2	3

Pretest, page 58

11. 6 **12.** 8 **13.** 4 **14.** 6 **15.** 6 **16.** 2

Lesson 5.1, page 59

	a	b	c	d	e	f
1.	7	4	9	6	5	7
2.	9	6	9	4	4	7
3.	9	5	6	8	4	5
4.	8	6	5	7	9	8
5.	6	6	8	5	3	3
6.	7	1	3	2	0	2

	a	b	c	d
7.	5	4	3	9

Lesson 5.2, page 60

	a	b	c	d	e	f
1.	7	9	6	8	9	7
2.	9	6	8	8	9	8
3.	8	6	1	8	0	9
4.	5	2	3	4	7	9
5.	4	5	5	6	3	4
6.	1	3	6	7	2	5

	a	b	c
7.	7	4	8

Lesson 5.3, page 61

	a	b	c	d	e	f
1.	8	5	3	8	4	6
2.	3	7	7	6	9	8
3.	7	8	2	6	4	4
4.	5	6	3	5	2	0
5.	1	5	6	7	9	7

	a	b	c
6.	7	8	9
7.	9	6	6

Lesson 5.4, page 62

	a	b	c	d	e
1.	7	4	9	7	6
2.	8	5	9	6	9
3.	6	7	4	6	9
4.	9	4	7	8	9
5.	8	3	4	7	5
6.	8	2	9	0	4

Lesson 5.5, page 63

1. 8 **2.** 5 **3.** 9 **4.** 4 **5.** 8 **6.** 7

Lesson 5.6, page 64

1. 8 **2.** 8 **3.** 5 **4.** 9 **5.** 9 **6.** 2

Posttest, page 65

	a	b	c	d	e
1.	6	3	1	8	8
2.	8	6	2	3	7
3.	5	8	6	7	4
4.	7	1	3	9	6
5.	4	5	4	7	6
6.	0	8	9	2	7
7.	4	6	8	8	6
8.	5	9	6	7	2
9.	5	7	7	3	8
10.	6	1	4	9	4

Posttest, page 66

11. 8 **12.** 3 **13.** 8 **14.** 9 **15.** 7 **16.** 9

Chapter 6

Pretest, page 67

	a	b	c	d	e
1.	21	7r1	71	21	60
2.	30r2	173r2	6r7	10	24r2
3.	9r6	11	25	87r1	300
4.	15	21	130	9r6	22r2
5.	181	20r1	8r6	3r1	45

Pretest, page 68

6. 2; 4 **7.** 78 **8.** 3 **9.** 15 **10.** 12 **11.** 47; 6

Spectrum Math
Grade 4

Answer Key

173

Grade 4 Answers

Grade 4 Answers

Lesson 6.1, page 69

	a	b	c	d	e
1.	5r1	8r2	7r3	9r1	5r5
2.	8r2	5r2	6r1	7r1	6r4
3.	3r3	8r1	3r1	9r1	8r1
4.	2r4	6r1	6r1	4r1	9r2

Lesson 6.1, page 70

	a	b	c	d	e
1.	18	15r1	11r2	24	13r2
2.	17r1	32	13	12	25
3.	15r3	12	11r1	12r5	11
4.	22	28	38r1	19r2	11r5

Lesson 6.2, page 71

	a	b	c	d	e
1.	31r1	15	10r7	12r4	11r1
2.	24	12	13	16r1	19r2
3.	37r1	8r2	15r3	11r1	34r1
4.	21r1	12r3	19	11r3	19r2
5.	14r3	11r5	24r1	14r1	12r1

Lesson 6.2, page 72

6. 8 7. 38 8. 2 9. 7 10. 23 ; 3

Lesson 6.3, page 73

	a	b	c	d	e
1.	90	93	41r3	43r1	75
2.	92	46r1	62	98r8	21
3.	86r6	45	90r3	73	36r2

Lesson 6.3, page 74

	a	b	c	d	e
1.	109r1	190r2	157r1	114r3	124r2
2.	311	114	115r1	225r1	150
3.	104	256	101r6	212	127
4.	417r1	176	109r3	126r2	142

Lesson 6.4, page 75

	a	b	c	d	e
1.	128r5	449	141r2	130r1	324
2.	158r1	183	109r8	128r1	197
3.	105r4	112r1	225r1	174	155
4.	261r1	157r3	160r1	111r3	305
5.	108	190r3	217	325	120

Lesson 6.4, page 76

6. 15 7. 168; 3 8. 58; 7 9. 130; 3 10. 146

Posttest, page 77

	a	b	c	d	e
1.	16	107	16r1	12r1	89
2.	30r1	133	111r2	106	111r1
3.	48	29	11r5	14	4r3
4.	9r3	9r1	5r3	9r8	22
5.	201	183r2	127	5r2	24

Posttest, page 78

6. 22; 4 7. 4 8. 123 9. 65 10. 68 11. 17

Mid-Test

Page 79

	a	b	c	d	e
1.	25	39	19	39	66
2.	19	74	89	59	79
3.	30	91	81	40	41
4.	43	65	94	81	33
5.	31	72	10	53	32
6.	66	84	9	55	19
7.	69	59	62	82	99
8.	49	93	80	75	65
9.	302	692	209	457	389
10.	889	479	283	462	589

Page 80

11a. 700 + 30 + 2

11b. 30,000 + 2000 + 100 + 30 + 2

11c. 4,000 + 700 + 90

12a. 1,000 + 3

12b. 2,000,000 + 300,000 + 10,000 + 4,000 + 700 + 30 + 2

12c. 3,000 + 1

	a	b	c
13.	13,600	80,000	2,000,000
14.	4,940	400,000	4,020

15a. 13,702 > 13,207 **15b.** 3,976 < 9362

15c. 932 > nine hundred-one

16a. 26,314 < 260,314 **16b.** 978 = 978

16c. 3,721,460 > 3,710,460

	a	b	c	d	e
17.	875	783	1,088	941	779
18.	3,032	2,350	4,606	9,115	9,810

Page 81

	a	b	c	d	e
19.	29,014	53,010	31,009	54,002	19,147
20.	8,411	24,810	4,095	28,999	16,949
21.	5,150	39,947	10,990	39,559	4,970
22.	91,710	4,464	49,930	8,378	79,967
23.	9,000	29,000	5,400	111,000	90,000
24.	31,000	1,000	39,100	10,000	9,000

Page 82

	a	b	c	d	e
25.	56	36	28	48	84
26.	96	28	88	48	80
27.	224	141	168	360	153
28.	336	576	336	175	441

	a	b	c	d	e	f
29.	110	242	992	860	500	620
30.	1,875	576	5,412	2,997	1,751	10,716
31.	18,810	16,000	9,353	13,294	46,124	7,581

Page 83

	a	b	c	d	e
32.	9	8	6	8	6
33.	3	7	4	9	8
34.	110	321	103	121	108
35.	90r4	91r2	105	41r1	438
36.	50r8	115r2	114	316r1	178r1
37.	100r8	255	162	111	74r1

Page 84

38. 36 **39.** 60 **40.** 210 **41.** 18 **42.** 80
43. 400

Chapter 7

Pretest, page 85

	a	b	c
1.	$\frac{3}{8}$	$\frac{4}{8}$	$\frac{1}{4}$
2.	$\frac{2}{5}$	$\frac{3}{6}$	$\frac{1}{6}$

	a	b	c	d
3.	$\frac{3}{4} > \frac{1}{4}$	$\frac{1}{2} = \frac{2}{4}$	$\frac{7}{8} > \frac{2}{8}$	$\frac{2}{8} < \frac{4}{8}$
4.	$\frac{2}{2}$	$\frac{5}{8}$	$\frac{2}{4}$	$\frac{3}{6}$
5.	$\frac{5}{8}$	$\frac{1}{4}$	$\frac{0}{7}$	$\frac{2}{4}$
6.	0.51	0.86	0.723	$7.75	$2.08
7.	0.44	0.31	$8.06	$75.13	0.093

Pretest, page 86

8. $\frac{2}{4}$ **9.** $\frac{2}{8}$ **10.** $\frac{5}{8}$ **11.** 50¢ **12.** $31.96
13. $1.07

Lesson 7.1, page 87

	a	b	c
1.	$\frac{1}{3}$	$\frac{2}{4}$	$\frac{5}{8}$
2.	$\frac{5}{10}$	$\frac{4}{5}$	$\frac{1}{2}$
3.	$\frac{2}{4}$	$\frac{1}{2}$	$\frac{1}{3}$

Lesson 7.2, page 88

	a	b	c
1.	$\frac{3}{10}$	$\frac{2}{4}$	$\frac{3}{6}$
2.	$\frac{1}{4}$	$\frac{1}{2}$	$\frac{4}{8}$
3.	$\frac{1}{3}$	$\frac{2}{3}$	$\frac{2}{5}$

Lesson 7.3, page 89

	a	b	c	d
1.	$\frac{3}{12} > \frac{2}{12}$	$\frac{3}{4} > \frac{1}{4}$	$\frac{5}{8} < \frac{6}{8}$	$\frac{1}{2} = \frac{1}{2}$
2.	$\frac{2}{3} > \frac{1}{3}$	$\frac{2}{10} < \frac{4}{10}$	$\frac{5}{8} > \frac{3}{8}$	$\frac{11}{12} > \frac{10}{12}$
3.	$\frac{4}{5} = \frac{4}{5}$	$\frac{7}{12} < \frac{8}{12}$	$\frac{6}{10} > \frac{5}{10}$	$\frac{3}{4} > \frac{2}{4}$
4.	$\frac{8}{12} > \frac{6}{12}$	$\frac{4}{5} = \frac{4}{5}$	$\frac{2}{4} > \frac{1}{4}$	$\frac{5}{8} < \frac{7}{8}$

Lesson 7.4, page 90

	a	b	c	d
1.	$\frac{9}{12}$	$\frac{4}{16}$	$\frac{10}{15}$	$\frac{2}{4}$
2.	$\frac{6}{18}$	$\frac{6}{24}$	$\frac{3}{15}$	$\frac{8}{40}$
3.	$\frac{10}{14}$	$\frac{12}{24}$	$\frac{8}{32}$	$\frac{6}{36}$
4.	$\frac{9}{27}$	$\frac{20}{30}$	$\frac{10}{25}$	$\frac{2}{16}$
5.	15	2	12	18
6.	4	16	24	6
7.	40	15	21	10
8.	8	20	27	9

Lesson 7.4, page 91

	a	b	c	d
1.	$\frac{1}{5}$	$\frac{4}{8}$	$\frac{1}{3}$	$\frac{1}{5}$
2.	$\frac{1}{6}$	$\frac{4}{5}$	$\frac{1}{5}$	$\frac{4}{5}$
3.	$\frac{3}{4}$	$\frac{7}{8}$	$\frac{1}{3}$	$\frac{1}{9}$
4.	$\frac{2}{5}$	$\frac{5}{6}$	$\frac{1}{2}$	$\frac{2}{3}$
5.	8	3	1	1
6.	9	2	5	4
7.	2	2	1	12
8.	7	5	8	1

Lesson 7.5, page 92

	a	b	c	d	e
1.	$\frac{11}{12}$	$\frac{3}{5}$	$\frac{5}{6}$	$\frac{3}{4}$	
2.	$\frac{4}{10}$	$\frac{5}{8}$	$\frac{2}{3}$	$\frac{4}{7}$	
3.	$\frac{4}{5}$	$\frac{9}{12}$	$\frac{9}{10}$	$\frac{4}{5}$	
4.	$\frac{5}{8}$	$\frac{7}{12}$	$\frac{2}{6}$	$\frac{3}{6}$	$\frac{2}{8}$
5.	$\frac{8}{12}$	$\frac{7}{7}$	$\frac{9}{10}$	$\frac{4}{5}$	$\frac{11}{12}$
6.	$\frac{8}{11}$	$\frac{2}{4}$	$\frac{2}{2}$	$\frac{6}{8}$	$\frac{4}{9}$

Lesson 7.6, page 93

	a	b	c	d	e
1.	$\frac{8}{12}$	$\frac{4}{10}$	$\frac{2}{4}$	$\frac{1}{7}$	$\frac{1}{5}$
2.	$\frac{2}{10}$	$\frac{1}{12}$	$\frac{2}{5}$	$\frac{3}{10}$	$\frac{4}{8}$
3.	$\frac{6}{10}$	$\frac{2}{11}$	$\frac{7}{9}$	$\frac{2}{5}$	$\frac{2}{9}$
4.	$\frac{2}{7}$	$\frac{4}{12}$	$\frac{1}{9}$	$\frac{4}{12}$	
5.	$\frac{2}{12}$	$\frac{1}{4}$	$\frac{2}{10}$	$\frac{7}{10}$	
6.	$\frac{4}{8}$	$\frac{1}{7}$	$\frac{3}{12}$	$\frac{7}{10}$	

Lesson 7.7, page 94

1. $\frac{2}{3}$ **2.** $\frac{1}{4}$ **3.** $\frac{4}{5}$ **4.** $\frac{6}{8}$ **5.** $\frac{5}{7}$ **6.** $\frac{5}{6}$

Grade 4 Answers

Lesson 7.8, page 95

	a	b	c
1.	hundredths	thousands	tenths
2.	tens	thousandths	tenths
3.	ones	hundredths	thousandths

	a	b	c	d
4.	4	1	5	2
5.	4	3	0	1
6.	3	2	5	1

Lesson 7.8, page 96

	a	b	c
1.	0.3 or $\frac{3}{10}$	0.7 or $\frac{7}{10}$	0.2 or $\frac{2}{10}$

	a	b	c	d
2.	0.2	0.6	0.9	0.4
3.	0.03	0.004	0.08	0.005

	a	b	c
4.	1.31 > 1.30	0.01 < 1.1	0.008 < 0.009
5.	1.32 < 1.42	1.3 > 1.03	0.66 < 0.67

Lesson 7.9, page 97

	a	b	c	d	e
1.	1.00	2.4	2.7	9.8	10.9
2.	10.2	8.6	18.67	23.12	15.15
3.	1.43	100.51	46.70	45.77	183.66
4.	500.62	111.00	562.15	113.35	200.90
5.	0.46	1.80	42.35	72.30	
6.	151.35	466.60	34.56	42.830	

Lesson 7.10, page 98

	a	b	c	d	e
1.	71.1	30.2	0.15	0.12	2.7
2.	235.11	85.99	1.187	53.326	93.10
3.	21.91	32.169	2.809	80.95	0.019
4.	7.312	28.602	1.199	0.893	1.80
5.	2.794	18.198	2.65	2.596	5.300
6.	2.206	2.195	33.656	56.80	40.81

Lesson 7.11, page 99

	a	b	c	d	e
1.	$20.41	$2.60	97¢	56¢	$11.80
2.	87¢	$18.20	$2192.63	$6.03	$1.30
3.	$610.05	$97.64	$900.32	$6348.13	$198.60
4.	$599.23	55¢	$95.80	$2553.03	33¢
5.	$89.01	$11.09	$23.07	16¢	$1133.95
6.	$136.78	87¢	$9.61	$560.90	$265.60

Lesson 7.11, page 100

1. $7.60   2. $580.15   3. $1.20   4. 90¢
5. $132.15   6. $4.75

Posttest, page 101

	a	b	c	d	e
1.	$\frac{10}{10}$	$\frac{8}{12}$	$\frac{7}{10}$	$\frac{2}{4}$	$\frac{6}{8}$
2.	0.60	51.83	15.324	$59.10	74¢
3.	1.4728	$2,027.56	0.013	1.10	$80.74
4.	20.070	$1,298.70	$1.64	10.110	128.63
5.	247.09	$55.80	0.004	0.085	$327.51
6.	$\frac{3}{12}$	$\frac{3}{9}$	$\frac{2}{10}$	$\frac{1}{4}$	$\frac{3}{8}$

7a. $0.32 > 0.23$ 7b. $\frac{11}{12} > \frac{3}{12}$ 7c. $0.4 = \frac{4}{10}$
7d. $0.015 < 0.105$

Posttest, page 102

8. 26.38   9. $\frac{11}{12}$ 10. $34.25   11. $31.05
12. $\frac{8}{12}$ 13. $0.10

Chapter 8

Pretest, page 103

1a. 1 yd.   1b. 2 gal.   2a. 8 oz.   2b. 1760 yd.
3a. 24 in.   3b. 5 pt.   4a. 1 yd.   4b. 4 qt.
5a. 20 c   5b. 2 qt.   6a. $1\frac{1}{2}$ in.   6b. 3 in.
7a. $2\frac{1}{2}$ in.   7b. 1 in.   8a. 70 in.   8b. 68 ft.
9a. 300 sq. yd.   9b. 72 sq. in.

Pretest, page 104

10. 12   11. 6 ft.   12. 1,000 lb.   13. 25 yd.
14. 80 sq. ft.

Lesson 8.1, page 105

1. 3 in.   2. $2\frac{1}{2}$ in.   3. $\frac{1}{2}$ in.
4.–9.   Lines should be the length specified.

Lesson 8.2, page 106

1. $2\frac{1}{4}$ in.   2. $\frac{3}{4}$ in.   3. $1\frac{1}{4}$ in.   4. $3\frac{1}{8}$ in.   5. $1\frac{1}{8}$ in.
6.–9.   Lines should be the length specified.

Lesson 8.3, page 107

	a	b	c
1.	15 ft.	96 in.	216 ft.
2.	4 ft.	5,280 yd.	864 in.
3.	1,000 yd.	2 ft.	10,560 ft.
4.	1 ft.	936 in.	4 yd.
5.	10 yd.	120 in.	2160 ft.
6.	12,320 yd.	200 ft.	108 yd.
7.	52,800 ft.	50 ft.	72 in.
8.	11 ft.	1,800 in.	3 ft.
9.	24 yd.	1 yd.	303 ft.
10.	14,080 yd.	16 yd.	10 ft.

Lesson 8.3, page 108

1. 60 in.   2. 3 yd.   3. 75 ft.   4. 12 yd.
5. 7,040 yd.   6. 780 ÷ 3 = 260 yd.
7. 10,000 ÷ 5,000 = 2 mi.

Grade 4 Answers

Lesson 8.4, page 109

	a	b	c
1.	8 qt.	2 qt.	6 pt.
2.	6 gal.	2 c.	20 pt.
3.	7 qt.	7 gal.	28 c.
4.	24 pt.	4 c.	7 pt.
5.	40 qt.	60 c.	9 pt.
6.	48 qt.	11 qt.	8 c.
7.	15 qt.	160 oz.	10 gal.
8.	9 pt.	88 c.	160 pt.
9.	300 pt.	100 pt.	320 oz.
10.	11 c.	4 gal.	100 pt.

Lesson 8.5, page 110

	a	b	c
1.	2 lb.	3 T.	8,000 lb.
2.	640 oz.	4 lb.	12 T.
3.	$\frac{1}{2}$ T.	$\frac{1}{2}$ lb.	9 T.
4.	128 oz.	192 oz.	5 T.

5. 10,000 lb. 6. 2 T. 7. 96,000 oz.
8. 128,000 oz. 9. 1 T. 10. 19,2000 oz.
11. 20,000 lb.

Lesson 8.6, page 111

1. 30 gal. 2. 40,000 lb. 3. 15,760 oz.
4. 300 qt. 5. 6,000 lb. 6. 3 gal.

Lesson 8.7, page 112

	a	b	c
1.	14 yd.	30 ft.	28 in.
2.	225 yd.	120 yd.	55 ft.
3.	42 ft.	34 in.	150 in.

Lesson 8.8, page 113

	a	b	c	d
1.	180 sq. in.	144 sq. ft.	132 sq. ft.	1,750 sq. in.
2.	250 sq. yd.	40 sq. in.	480 sq. yd.	
3.	184 sq. yd.	80 sq. ft.		

Lesson 8.9, page 114

1. 100 ft. 2. 600 sq. ft. 3. 4,125 sq. ft. 4. 52 ft.
5. 625 sq. ft. 6. 306 ft. 7. 18,750 sq. ft.

Posttest, page 115

	a	b	c
1.	$1\frac{1}{2}$ in.	$1\frac{1}{4}$ in.	
2.	$\frac{1}{2}$ in.	$1\frac{1}{8}$ in.	
3.	48 in.	80 oz.	4,000 lb.
4.	1 gal.	9 c.	45 ft.
5.	3 mi.	34 c.	5 lb.
6.	44 ft.	45 yd.	
7.	300 sq. ft.	225 sq. in.	

Posttest, page 116

8. 4 gal. 9. 120 c. 10. 2 lb. 11. 800 oz.
12. 7,920 ft. 13. 160 oz.

Chapter 9

Pretest, page 117

1. 5,000 m; 60 L 2. 600 cm; 32,000 g
3. 720 mm; 19000 mL 4. 1000 mg; 1 m
5. 25,000 g; 650 mm 6. 17000 mL; 52 m
7. 7 g; 25,000 m 8. 20 cm; 9 L 9. 3 cm; 5 cm
10. 1 cm; 10 cm 11. 20 mm; 10 mm
12. 40 mm; 50 mm

Pretest, page 118

13. 35,000 m 14. 1,000 g 15. 30 L 16. 52 g
17. 564 m

Lesson 9.1, page 119

1. 2 cm; 1 cm 2. 4 cm; 3 cm
3. 8 cm; 3 cm 4. 10 cm; 5 cm
5.–8. Answers should be drawn in length specified.

Lesson 9.2, page 120

1. 20 mm; 30 mm 2. 50 mm; 90 mm
3. 70 mm; 20 mm 4. 50 mm; 6 cm
5. 9 cm; 110 mm 6. 10 cm; 250 mm

Lesson 9.3, page 121

1.–7. Answers will vary. 8. 6 m; 9 km
9. 700 cm; 10 km 10. 7,000 m; 23,000 m
11. 800 cm; 3200 cm 12. 2,000 m; 1400 cm

Lesson 9.4, page 122

1. 400 cm; 2,500 mm 2. 21,000 m; 2,500 mm
3. 3,300 cm; 14,000 m 4. 1,500 cm; 47,000 mm
5. 5,000 m; 840 mm 6. 7,500 cm; 7,200 cm
7. 10,000 m; 66,000 mm 8. 210 mm; 19,000 m

Lesson 9.5, page 123

1. 23 cm; 23 mm; 30 m 2. 27 m; 16 cm; 30 mm
3. 6 cm; 9 cm 4. 80 mm; 80 mm

Lesson 9.6, page 124

	a	b	c
1.	60 sq. mm	16 sq. m	14 sq. cm
2.	105 sq. m	70 sq. cm	54 sq. mm
3.	276 sq. m	51 sq. cm	80 sq. mm
4.	100 sq. m	168 sq. cm	25 sq .mm

Lesson 9.7, page 125

1. 3,000 mL ; 12,000 mL ; 2,000 mL
2. 75,000 mL ; 10,000 mL ; 50,000 mL
3. 13,000 mL ; 78,000 mL ; 8,000 mL
4. 75,000 mL 5. 7 L 6. 12

Grade 4 Answers

Lesson 9.8, page 126
1. 60,00 g; 32,000 mg; 45,000 g
2. 10,000 mg; 42,000 g; 9,000 mg
3. 105,000 mg; 37,000 mg; 12,000 g
4. 183,000 g; 18,000 mg; 119,000 g
5. 45 g **6.** 7 g

Posttest, page 127
1. 60 cm; 20500 mm **2.** 130 mm; 400 cm
3. 37,000 m; 15,000 mL **4.** 44,000 mg; 9,000 g
5. 9,500 cm; 2,200 mm **6.** 5 km ; 7,600 cm
7. 5,600 cm; 232,000 m **8.** 8,650 mm; 45000 mL
9. 267,000 mg; 26,000 g **10.** 2,000 mL; 150 mm
11. 22,000 mm; 67,000 m **12.** 3 m; 3 km
13. 20 mm; 70 cm **14.** 29 km; 26 m

Posttest, page 128
15. 100 sq. km; 560 sq. cm
16. 99 sq. m; 45 sq. mm **17.** 8,000 mL
18. 75,000 m

Chapter 10

Pretest, page 129
1. Sat. **2.** $17 **3.** increases **4.** 10 lb. **5.** 30 lb.
6. T **7.** T **8.** T

Pretest, page 130
9. $\frac{1}{8}$ **10.** $\frac{2}{8}$ **11.** $\frac{5}{15}$

Lesson 10.1, page 131
1. pizza **2.** F **3.** T **4.** bear **5.** F **6.** T

Lesson 10.1, page 132
1. rap and rock **2.** F **3.** F **4.** T **5.** football
6. 10 **7.** soccer **8.** F **9.** T **10.** T

Lesson 10.2, page 133
1. wk 4 **2.** wks 2 and 3 **3.** Feb. **4.** 3

Lesson 10.2, page 134
1. June **2.** 8 **3.** F **4.** F **5.** Jan. **6.** F **7.** F
8. F **9.** T

Lesson 10.3, page 135
1. $\frac{2}{16}$ **2.** $\frac{4}{8}$ **3.** $\frac{3}{5}$ **4.** $\frac{0}{5}$

Lesson 10.3, page 136
1. $\frac{10}{35}$ **2.** $\frac{1}{4}$ **3.** $\frac{1}{15}$; unlikely **4.** $\frac{25}{100}$; unlikely

Posttest, page 137
1. third **2.** $6 **3.** F **4.** T **5.** gerbils **6.** F
7. F **8.** T

Posttest, page 138
9. $\frac{5}{8}$ **10.** $\frac{1}{8}$ **11.** $\frac{0}{8}$ **12.** $\frac{1}{7}$; unlikely

Chapter 11

Pretest, page 139
1a. hexagon **1b.** triangle
1c. quadrilateral **1d.** pentagon
2a. square pyramid **2b.** cube
2c. rectangular prism **2d.** cylinder
3. flip; turn; slide
4. not congruent ; congruent; not congruent

Pretest, page 140
5. ray; line; vertex **6.** line segment; point
7. acute; right; obtuse
8. parallel; perpendicular; perpendicular
9.
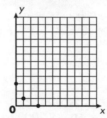
10. A (3, 2); B (0, 0); C (2, 3)

Lesson 11.1, page 141

	a	b	c
1.	octagon	nonagon	pentagon
2.	triangle	hexagon	quadrilateral

Lesson 11.2, page 142
1a. cone **1b.** pentagon **1c.** triangle **1d.** hexagon
2a. sphere **2b.** cylinder
2c. quadrilateral **2d.** triangle
3a. cube **3b.** rectangular solid
3c. heptagon **3d.** quadrilateral

Lesson 11.3, page 143

	a	b	c
1.	congruent	not congruent	not congruent
2.	not congruent	congruent	congruent
3.	not congruent	congruent	congruent
4.	not congruent	congruent	congruent

Lesson 11.4, page 144

	a	b	c
1.	flip	turn	slide
2.	flip	slide	flip
3.	flip	slide	flip

Lesson 11.5, page 145

	a	b	c	d
1.	line	vertex	point	line segment
2.	ray	ray	line segment	vertex
3.	↔	↗	•—•	↖↗

Grade 4 Answers

4.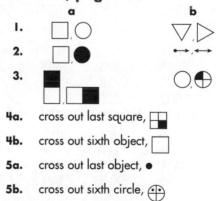

	a	b	c

5. □△○   ◇◯⬡

6. ●◢◼

Lesson 11.6, page 146

	a	b	c
1.	right	obtuse	right
2.	acute	acute	obtuse
3.	obtuse	right	acute
4.	obtuse	acute	right

Lesson 11.7, page 147

1a. perpendicular   **1b.** parallel
1c. perpendicular   **1d.** intersecting
2a. parallel   **2b.** intersecting
2c. perpendicular   **2d.** parallel
3a. intersecting   **3b.** perpendicular
3c. parallel   **3d.** intersecting
4a. perpendicular   **4b.** parallel
4c. intersecting   **4d.** perpendicular

Lesson 11.8, page 148

	a	b	c
1.	(3, 3)	(8, 2)	(2, 4)
2.	(3, 2)	(2, 3)	(5, 5)

Posttest, page 149

	a	b	c
1.	quadrilateral	triangle	pentagon
2.	heptagon	hexagon	triangle
3.	cube	sphere	rectangular prism
4.	cone	cylinder	square pyramid
5.	not congruent	congruent	not congruent

Posttest, page 150

6. slide ; flip ; turn
7. (4, 5) ; (6, 3) ; (0, 7)

	a	b	c	d
8.	ray	vertex	line segment	line
9.	acute	right	obtuse	acute
10.	parallel	perpendicular	intersecting	perpendicular

Chapter 12

Pretest, page 151

	a	b
1.	3, 5, 2	30, 10, 40
2.	50, 25, 10	5, 1, 3
3.	25, 30, 35	504, 502, 500
4.	64, 128, 256	132, 177

5. □△○   ◇◯⬡

6. ●◢◼   1, 1, 1

Pretest, page 152

	a	b	c
7.	6	30	8
8.	25	2	125
9.	6	5	
10.	235	2	
11.	75 ÷ 3 = 25		
12.	96 − 4 = 92		

Lesson 12.1, page 153

	a	b
1.	7, 4	1, 300, 200
2.	23, 78	100, 30, 2
3.	24, 45, 36	100, 10, 200
4.	36, 6	22, 52
5.	230	15, 13, 15
6.	750	960, 11

Lesson 12.2, page 154

	a	b
1.	41, 50	39, 72
2.	11	388
3.	25, 47	138, 128, 116
4.	808	308, 418
5.	400, 310	873, 853
6.	120	116
7.	50, 55	12, 26

Lesson 12.3, page 155

	a	b
1.	□, ○	▽, ▷
2.	□, ●	↔, ↔
3.		○, ⊕

4a. cross out last square, ⊟
4b. cross out sixth object, □
5a. cross out last object, ●
5b. cross out sixth circle, ⊕

Lesson 12.4, page 156

	a	b	c
1.	6	3	764
2.	153	17	39
3.	1250	25	5
4.	6	690	32
5.	12	2	50

Grade 4 Answers

Lesson 12.5, page 157
1. 2; 135 2. 190; 5 3. 25; 25
4. 1245; 130 5. 20; 15 6. 25; 32

Lesson 12.5, page 158
1. $63 \times 7 = 441$ 2. $182 \times 2 = 364$
3. $58 \div 29 = 2$
4. $\$12.32 \times 5 = \$61.60$
5. $\$17.50 + \$18.50 + \$12.50 = \$48.50$

Posttest, page 159

	a	b
1.	24, 23	256, 259
2.	33, 22	488, 441, 416
3.	82, 104	21, 33
4.	⊘,⊘	▱,▢
5.	◕,▦,▧	

Posttest, page 160
6. 3 ; 75 7. 5 ; 6 8. 6 ; 20
9. $\$2.45 - \$1.13 = \$1.32$
10. $15 + 25 + 2 = 42$

Final Test

Page 161

	a	b	c	d	e
1.	36	1,964	790	285	1,054
2.	4,330	980	12,750	1,055	3,659
3.	31,168	11,122	27,760	21,688	67,123
4.	91	79	48	39	53
5.	527	5,269	1,532	2,136	455
6.	429	1,281	754	2,007	818

Page 162

	a	b	c	d	e
7.	702	448	873	384	225
8.	9,604	1,170	1,728	4,158	2,241
9.	25,272	7,002	10,320	7,904	39,702
10.	295,470	84,126	270,096	142,344	122,500
11.	15	8	16r2	18r4	17
12.	82r1	291	125	197r2	100
13.	371r1	2641	938r3	2409r1	503
14.	1638r4	625	1400r4	730r1	1,230

Page 163
15. tenths; ten thousands
16. thousandths; hundreds
17. 103,500; 2,000,000
18. 23,000; 580
19. $14.05 < 14.95$; $12700 < 12,703$;
$164,000 > 146,000$

20. $17.05 = 17.05$; $0.008 < 0.010$;
$0.010 < 0.100$

	a	b	c	d	e
21.	1,000	220,000	3,880	64,000	9,000
22.	$\frac{6}{6}$	$\frac{10}{12}$	$\frac{2}{8}$	$\frac{4}{12}$	
23.	1	4	25	56	

Page 164

	a	b	c	d
24.	$19.64	0.051	50¢	7.722
25.	1 yd.	70 mm	10000 lb.	
26.	6 pt.	72,000 g	44 yd.	
27.	20,000 mm	14,000 m	22,000 mL	
28.	11 ft.	40 in.	44 m	

29. 150 sq. ft.; 176 sq. cm; 300 sq. in.; 2050 sq. cm
30. cupcakes; 15

Page 165
31. $\frac{3}{8}$; $\frac{0}{8}$
32a. cube
32b. rectangle
32c. cylinder
32d. pentagon
32e. triangle
33a. line segment
33b. ray
33c. right angle
33d. obtuse angle
33e. acute angle

	a	b	c
34.	intersecting	perpendicular	parallel
35.	54	97, 112	
36.	1,095	0, 50, 125	

Page 166
37. A (5, 4); B (9, 1); C (0, 0); D (5, 0); E (0, 8)

	a	b
38.	21	22
39.	5	10
40.	30	3

41. $1760 \times 10 = 17600$
42. $28 \times 3 = 84$